Perfect Numerical Test Results

Kenexa® is a global human capital management firm that helps organizations recruit and retain talented people. Kenexa solutions include a wide range of psychometric and skills assessments, applicant tracking, employment process outsourcing, phone screening, structured interviews, performance management, multi-rater feedback surveys, employee engagement surveys and HR Analytics.

The book's authors are all employees within the Kenexa Assessment practice, based in London. Between them they have over 50 years of experience designing and analysing psychometric assessments across a wide range of industry sectors and for a range of applications, such as selection, development and career counselling.

This book was written by
Dr Joanna Moutafi, C. Psychol.
Sarah Mortenson, MSc
Ian Newcombe, C. Psychol., AFBPsS
Sean Keeley, C. Psychol.
Mark Abrahams, MSc

Other titles in the *Perfect* series

Perfect Answers to Interview Questions – Max Eggert
Perfect Babies' Names – Rosalind Fergusson
Perfect Best Man – George Davidson
Perfect CV – Max Eggert
Perfect Interview – Max Eggert
Perfect Personality Profiles – Helen Baron
Perfect Psychometric Test Results – Joanna Moutafi and Ian Newcombe
Perfect Pub Quiz – David Pickering
Perfect Punctuation – Stephen Curtis
Perfect Readings for Weddings – Jonathan Law
Perfect Wedding Speeches and Toasts – George Davidson

Perfect
Numerical Test
Results

Joanna Moutafi
Sarah Mortenson
Ian Newcombe
Sean Keeley
Mark Abrahams

BOOKS

Published by Random House Books 2007

2 4 6 8 10 9 7 5 3 1

Copyright © Kenexa 2007

The authors have asserted their right
under the Copyright, Designs and Patents Act 1988
to be identified as the authors of this work

First published in the United Kingdom in 2007 by
Random House Books

Random House Books
Random House, 20 Vauxhall Bridge Road,
London SW1V 2SA

www.randomhouse.co.uk

Addresses for companies within The Random House Group Limited can be found at:
www.randomhouse.co.uk/offices.htm

The Random House Group Limited Reg. No. 954009

A CIP catalogue record for this book
is available from the British Library

ISBN 9781905211333

The Random House Group Limited makes every effort to ensure that the papers used
in its books are made from trees that have been legally sourced from well-managed
and credibly certified forests. Our paper procurement policy can be found at:
www.randomhouse.co.uk/paper.htm

Typeset by Palimpsest Book Production Limited, Grangemouth, Stirlingshire
Printed in the UK by CPI Bookmarque, Croydon CR0 4TD

Contents

Preface

If you are looking at this book you have probably been asked to complete a numerical test. Perhaps you are applying for jobs and going for interviews, or perhaps you are doing a training course within your company. Either way, you've come to the right place. This book is designed to help you face the test, and it contains everything you need to get the highest mark possible.

The first part of the book explains every aspect of numerical tests, and it answers any questions you might have about why they are set and how they are scored. It also includes a section on online testing, which more and more employers are using. The next section of the book is all about improving your performance. It's packed full of tips on how to relax before taking the test, advice about overcoming anxiety or stress, and hints about how to make sure you perform to the very best of your ability. The final section contains plenty of practice questions, written by the expert team at Kenexa. With them, you can hone your skills and prepare yourself for the types of challenges you will face.

After reading this book, you will

- Have a better understanding of numerical tests.
- Be familiar with all the different types of numerical test questions.
- Have a clear idea of how the testing process works.
- Be confident when faced with any numerical test.

More and more jobseekers and employees are being asked to take numerical tests, and some people find the whole process very daunting, but with a bit of background knowledge and some practice there is no reason why you should not be able to complete numerical tests to the best of your abilities.

1 Introduction to numerical tests

What are numerical tests?

Numerical tests, also called numerical reasoning tests, are a type of psychometric test. Each psychometric test is designed to measure an aspect of a person's ability or behaviour in a structured way. Unsurprisingly, numerical tests are designed to measure your numerical ability or, to put it more simply, your head for numbers.

Companies that are recruiting for positions in finance, accounting, engineering and other mechanical fields are extremely likely to use a numerical test as part of their selection process – after all, these jobs entail dealing with numbers every day. But many other occupations, if not all, require at least some basic skills with numbers, and so numerical tests are an increasingly important component in recruitment for lots of different sectors. Not only that, they are also always used in large-scale graduate recruitment processes.

Why are numerical tests used?

Numerical tests are used to find out how well a candidate will be able to deal with the aspect of the job that requires some ability with numbers. On their own, of course, numerical tests won't tell employers that much about a person's ability to do a job well. A candidate could get a brilliant score on a numerical test but still be completely unsuited to the job. Most jobs, after all, require some 'soft skills', such as getting on with people and being organized, and a numerical test is not designed to detect these. As part of a whole recruitment process, however, numerical tests can be extremely useful. Interviews and references give employers a broad idea of what someone is like, but there is nothing like a numerical test for hard information on how someone deals with numbers.

How are numerical tests scored?

The most usual way for numerical tests to be scored is in relation to the number of questions answered correctly. For example, if you answered 20 out of 25 questions correctly, your score would be 20. Other numerical tests, however, use a much more complex procedure to generate a score. Some factors that are often taken into account, in various combinations, are:

- the length of time taken over each question;
- the number of mistakes made;
- the level of difficulty of the answered questions;
- whether or not the candidate could have guessed the answer.

As you will never know for certain how a test is being scored, the best strategy to adopt is always to try to answer as many questions correctly as you can. No matter which scoring methods or formulae are used, the number of correctly answered questions will always be taken into consideration – so the best thing you can do for your final score is to get as many right answers as you can.

What do test scores mean?

Let's look again at the example of the numerical test for which you scored 20 out of a possible 25. What does this tell you about your numerical reasoning ability? The answer is, not much at all! For your results to have some meaning they will need to be compared with the results achieved by a specially selected group of people. This group, known as a population, is made up of lots of other people who work in a similar position to the one you're applying for. When you receive feedback from a numerical reasoning test, you will get your percentile score or grade but not your actual score.

Percentiles are not the same as percentages. A percentile is a number between 1 and 100, and it tells you the percentage of the population who took the test and scored lower than you. For example, if your score of 20 corresponded to a percentile of 70 – that is, the 70th percentile – you scored a higher mark than 70 per cent of the population. Another way of saying this is that your score was in the top 30 per cent of the population.

The grading system of scores is a simpler version of the percentile scoring system. It gives you a picture of how you did in relation to the population that completed the test. This is how percentiles and grades are related:

Percentile	Grade	Description
90–99th percentile	A	well above average
70–89th percentile	B	above average
31–69th percentile	C	typical of the population
11–30th percentile	D	below average
0–10th percentile	E	well below average

What score do you need to pass?

At first glance, you might think that it would be helpful to know how well you need to do in order to pass. There are, however, disadvantages to this. For example, if you know that a test has a 'low' pass mark you might feel more confident, but this could lead you to become complacent and not put in enough preparation time. On the other hand, if you discover that the test requires a fairly 'high' pass mark, this may make you more tense and nervous, which will affect your performance. Therefore, the best thing you can do is not think about the pass mark and instead concentrate on doing your best.

It might be reassuring to know that more often than not employers are not trying to select the people with the best abilities so much as deselect those with the lowest abilities. It is quite common for organizations to use numerical tests to deselect up to 30 per cent of their applicants (though this depends largely on the specific role). So, as with every other aspect of job applications, whether you pass the numerical test stage depends on the other applicants.

The simple rule of numerical tests is that no score equates directly to a pass mark. How you do will depend on the other people applying and on the group to which you are being compared. So the best tactic is to forget about the passing mark and just think about doing your best.

Can practice improve your score?

Thankfully, the answer is 'yes'. Numerical tests are made up of lots of different types of questions, and practice will familiarize you with the sorts of things that are asked and the forms in which numerical data can appear. Studies have shown that no matter what level of natural ability people possess, everyone benefits from practising before a test. That's the good news. The bad news is that if you are not naturally mathematically minded, practice will help you achieve the best result you can, but it won't make you an overnight maths genius. Intelligence is something we are born with, and the best we can do is work hard to achieve our full potential. It's worth remembering, however, that if you put in the extra work and practise hard, you could still do better than someone who is naturally better with numbers but who hasn't put in the same amount of preparation as you.

In short, practising numerical questions will improve your score on a numerical test, but the amount of difference it makes will depend on your natural ability.

What are the standards for numerical tests?

To put it another way, how can you be sure that the tests you are asked to take are fair? There are rigorous assessment standards for numerical tests, all geared towards finding out whether each test is reliable and valid.

Reliability

A test is reliable if the scores it gives are consistent. It's important that someone sitting the test would get the same mark today as they would five months from now. This may seem a strange point to make – after all, numerical tests deal with right and wrong answers, so how could someone get different scores from one occasion to the next? Well, consider the different ways of calculating scores. Some tests time how long it takes candidates to answer questions and use this to help generate the score. Others assess how easy the questions answered were and weight the score according to whether or not the candidate could have guessed the answer. The complications are added to the formula for calculating the score, so it becomes more likely that there will be inconsistencies. All tests will have been formally checked for consistency because a test that does not give consistent results is useless.

Validity

A test is valid if it measures what it is supposed to measure. Numerical tests need to measure numerical ability, verbal reasoning tests need to measure verbal reasoning ability and so on. But how do you find out if a test assesses someone's ability? The best way is to follow the performance of someone who has taken the test and see if it matches up to the predictions of the test. Several studies have followed people who did well in recruitment numerical tests, seen how they performed in the job and compared them with people who didn't do so well in the tests. People who scored highly on numerical tests consistently performed better in several aspects of their jobs, and there is a growing body of evidence to suggest that numerical tests are the best indicator of potential in many different areas.

There are currently no laws governing the reliability or validity of tests. However, organizations do avoid using tests that have little or no reliability or validity because there would be no point in using them. Why would any organization spend a significant amount of money on a test that won't predict job performance? The specific requirements for good validity and reliability and how to measure these concepts are too involved to discuss here, but if you would like more information and a good introduction to the topic you could read the book *Reliability and Validity Assessment* by Edward Carmines and Richard Zeller.

The main reason for bringing up the concepts of validity and reliability here is so that you know you can trust numerical tests. It is worth remembering that your attitude towards the test may affect your performance. For example, if you thought that a test was made up by someone who was brilliant at maths for the sole purpose of making the job process difficult for you, you might feel disheartened and frustrated when completing the test. This could make it more difficult for you to concentrate, and you might, therefore, perform less well. However, if you understand that the tests are fair in that they predict who will perform better on the job, you might have a more positive attitude towards the testing process. This will mean that you will be more likely to perform to the best of your ability.

Do numerical tests discriminate?

The simple answer to this is 'yes'. Numerical tests are designed to discriminate between people with different levels of numerical ability. Despite the negative connotations of discrimination, the word only means finding differences between people – and these differences are not always negative. Every employer needs to distinguish between good and poor performers in order to select the right person for the job, and the question should really be whether numerical reasoning tests discriminate unfairly.

Unfair discrimination

The aim of every employer is to pick the most suitable person for a job. If candidates are chosen based on an ability that is needed for the role the test is discriminating fairly between them. Unfair discrimination, on the other hand, is to select a person for a job using either personal characteristics or abilities that have no relevance to the role. This unfair discrimination can be of two types: direct and indirect.

Direct discrimination

Direct discrimination refers to the selection of a person for a job role based on characteristics that are irrelevant to the position. This type of discrimination is illegal, and there are several Acts in place that regulate equal opportunities in the selection process. These include:

- Sex Discrimination Act 1986
- Race Relations Act 1976
- Disability Discrimination Act 1995
- Employment Equality Regulations 2003
- Age Discrimination Act 2006

Indirect discrimination

Indirect discrimination occurs when an organization does not employ an individual because of a characteristic that indirectly causes discrimination against a group of people. For example, if a company selects individuals for a position in the accounts department according to height, this could indirectly discriminate against women, who are typically shorter than men. Such unjustified discrimination is illegal.

However, indirect discrimination that is justified can be acceptable. For example, if the position was not in accountancy but in a basketball team, selecting individuals by height could be justified. Therefore, companies should discriminate between individuals only on the basis of characteristics that are relevant to the job requirements.

Issues to consider

Do you have a disability?

The Disability Discrimination Act prevents employers from directly discriminating against any applicants on the basis of their disability, and if you do have any form of disability you are protected against discrimination when you apply for a job. If you have a disability that could affect your performance in a numerical test, this is another thing to consider. People who set tests are aware that people may have disabilities, and there are various arrangements that can usually be made for you to complete the test in a different format.

If, for example, you have a motor disability that makes it difficult for you to get to the testing centre it might be possible for you to complete the test at an alternative location, perhaps even at your home. If you have a disability that affects your ability to use a keyboard you might be able to complete a pencil and paper version of the test. Similarly, if you have a visual or hearing impairment arrangements could be made for you to complete the test in an alternative form. Disabilities such as dyslexia may entitle you to have extra time when you are taking the test.

Because alternative arrangements will need to be made in these circumstances it is a good idea to give the recruiters plenty of notice.

Is English not your first language?

If English is not your first language and you are applying for a position in an English-speaking country it is possible that you will still be expected to take a numerical test in English. In general, if a job itself requires a good use of English you are unlikely to be given the test in an alternative language. If this is the case, you should inform the test administrator that you are not answering the test in your first language. It is important that the recruiters know your circumstances so that they can be taken into consideration during the decision-making process.

Will the fact that English is not your first language affect your test score? Unfortunately, the answer to this is that it depends on your fluency in English. In general, however, numerical tests do not use particularly complex or difficult language or vocabulary because they are tests of numerical reasoning ability and not tests of reading comprehension.

This relates back to the validity of the test: if the language of the test affected your ability to perform well the test would be measuring reading comprehension and not numerical ability. Therefore, it would not be measuring what it is supposed to measure and would have low, if any, validity.

What will the testing procedure be like?

If you are invited to complete a numerical test you might have to go into the office or to a specialist testing centre. Alternatively, you could be invited to complete a test online, which we will consider in the following section.

Ability tests are administered under exam conditions. You will typically be taking the test as part of a group, which usually includes between 10 and 30 people. There will be an administrator, who will begin by explaining the procedure in detail, probably by reading it from a script. The script might sound a little unnatural, but it is used to make sure that participants in different testing sessions receive the same information. After the administrator has explained the procedure, they will read the test instructions. Listen very carefully to these. If you are in doubt about anything the administrator says, make sure you ask before the testing session begins. Once the session has started, the administrator will not be allowed to answer any questions.

The testing session will be timed, and when the time is up you will be asked to stop writing. You might receive a warning 5 minutes or 1 minute before the time is up, but this will vary from test to test. Administrators are very strict with timing so that no participant has an unfair advantage. It is a good idea to take a watch with you and to keep track of the time so that you can finish as many questions as you possibly can.

What are online tests?

Online tests are completed on a computer and accessed through the internet. More and more employers are taking this option because it is much easier to organize. Not going to a testing session or being supervised while you take the test can have advantages. You will, for instance, be taking the test on home turf and in your own time, and you can make yourself as comfortable as you like and choose a time when you will perform at your best.

Differences between online and offline tests

Even though online and offline tests are considered to be equivalent, there are differences between the two:

- The conditions under which you complete the tests are different.
- You won't be able to ask any questions if you are taking a test online.

- There is typically only one version of an offline test, so all applicants complete the same version, whereas there are several equivalent versions of an online test.
- Online tests may be affected by your PC capabilities and internet connection.

Create the best testing conditions for you

When you take a normal psychometric test in a testing site you have no control over the conditions because they are standardized. When you take an online test, however, you can create your own conditions. Ideally, of course, you want to set up the sort of conditions that will help you perform to the best of your ability. This is what you should do.

- Choose to complete the test at a time of day when you are usually more alert. For most people, this will be during the morning.
- Try to make sure that nothing will distract you. Ask people who are at home with you not to disturb you, turn off your phone, sign out of your email and messenger accounts, and turn off any music and any appliances that create white noise in the background.
- Try to make sure that the room temperature is neither too high nor too low. A slightly cooler temperature will help you maintain alertness.
- Make sure the room is well lit.
- Wear comfortable clothing.
- Make sure that you have any equipment that you might need, such as paper and pencil or a calculator.
- Do not drink, eat or smoke during the test. This will distract you and waste valuable time.
- Remember that ability tests are timed, and in online tests you will not be warned when your time is running out. There will typically be a countdown clock on your screen while you are taking the test,

and you should check this occasionally but not so often that you lose your concentration.

What if I have a question when I am taking an online test?

Although there is no administrator who can answer your questions when you are completing a test online, you do have the advantage of being able to go through the instructions for as long as you require before you start the test. Bear in mind that the test setters know that you won't be able to ask anyone for clarification if you don't understand anything, so they will have taken great pains to present the instructions in such detail that you shouldn't need to ask any questions. If you really don't understand something crucial, you could contact the person who asked you to complete the test. This should be your last resort, however, because showing that you aren't able to understand detailed instructions might not give the best impression. If you really are stumped, remember that the issue you're unsure about may well become obvious as you start to take the test.

How do online test setters make sure people don't cheat?

Online tests have a time limit, but this wouldn't stop someone from cheating if they were really determined. One measure that is often employed is to create different versions of the test. There are two ways of making a new version of a test. The first is to create a parallel form; the second is to derive each new test from one 'bank' of items (questions).

Parallel forms
Parallel forms of a test are different tests that have an equal number of questions, with each test having the same properties as any other test. This means that all the versions have the same reliability and validity and they are designed so that a person will receive a similar score no matter which version they complete.

Item banks

Item-banked tests are created out of a large 'bank' of questions (items) with known properties. Because the properties of each question are known, they can be compared with each other and grouped into equivalent tests. This means that two item-banked versions of a test will have an equal number of questions, and each question in the first test will have equivalent properties to its corresponding question in the second test. Therefore, rather than having just equivalent tests, item-banked tests have equivalent questions.

Because the properties of each question are known, all the questions with the same properties can be used interchangeably in any test version. This means that when you are creating a test you have more combinations of questions you can use so that the probability of a candidate receiving the same test as someone else is very low. Item-banked tests are used in order to reduce the chances of cheating.

Item-banked tests are created through a sophisticated statistical procedure called Item Response Theory, which is far beyond the scope of this book. If you are interested in reading about this further *Fundamentals of Item Response Theory* by Ronald Hambleton, H. Swaminathan and H. Jane Rogers would be a good introductory read.

Technical considerations

Online tests are inevitably affected by the state of your computer and your internet connection, so how can you be sure that you will have no problems while you are taking the test?

PC specifications

When you are asked to complete an online test you will be sent an invitation. Read this carefully because it will typically include details of the PC specifications that are necessary for the test to run properly. You should check that your PC's specifications match those required before you take the test. Some tests have an in-built mechanism that automatically checks whether the PC specifications are appropriate and will not allow you to take the test if they are not.

If you experience any problems you should contact the person who sent you the invitation to complete the test. You might be experiencing problems because of a setting in your computer, in which case they should be able to talk you through it. Alternatively, if your PC does not meet the required specifications you will have to complete the test on a different PC.

Internet requirements

The internet connection requirements will be specified at the same time as the PC specifications. Test developers are, of course, aware that you may be using a computer that is old or slow and that your internet connection may not be very fast. Online tests are, therefore, generally designed to be accessible by at least 99 per cent of users. Again, if you do encounter a problem with accessing the test or while you are taking the test, contact the person who sent you the invitation and they should be able to help you.

At this point we have to warn you about something so that you don't fall into a not-so-uncommon trap. If you start taking the test but want to stop halfway through, don't just turn off your computer or close the program and then pretend that the internet connection was interrupted or that your PC crashed. It is easy for most test programmers to track your signal back and work out what caused your test to shut down, so you won't fool anyone. The golden rule is: start the test only when you feel totally ready to do so because you are unlikely to be able to quit a test once you have started it.

What if I can't get online?

If you do not have a PC or an internet connection it is not a good idea to get back to the recruiter to ask what alternatives there are. Performing well in any job means overcoming simple problems, and there are enough accessible PCs in libraries and internet cafés for you to be able to find a solution. If you have the opportunity, see if you can use a friend's computer, which will give you more control over your environment while you are taking the test.

2 Improve your performance

The best ways to improve your performance in numerical tests are to find out how the questions work and to practise solving a few, but there are a few other changes you can make and tips you can follow that could make a difference. Here is a quick and easy checklist of things to consider when you're preparing for a test.

Before the test

Familiarization and practice

Familiarizing yourself with numerical tests is the first step to success. You will need to get to know what the tests will look like, what they will measure and what the testing conditions will be. Once all these are clear, you need to practise.

Make sure you start working towards improving your performance a few days before your test date. This will have two main benefits. First, sleep is extremely good for your memory, and if you have the opportunity to get some sleep after learning something you will notice it really helps it lodge in your memory.

Second, you need to give yourself enough time to see the improvement in your scores. This will boost your confidence and make sure your anxiety remains under control during the test.

Anxiety

Anxiety affects different people in different ways. Some people get extremely nervous under testing conditions, and so they make mistakes. Others find that a bit of nervous energy really gets them going and slightly improves their performance. Still others seem able to look completely relaxed throughout the process – although it's quite likely they're hiding their nerves.

So what is it about numerical tests that makes us feel nervous? To begin with, the tests have important consequences. Whether you get a job could depend on the results you achieve. Equally, not knowing exactly what questions will come up can be nerve racking. And finally, the thought that you are going to be judged by your answers might be a cause for concern: few of us like being judged, and no one likes to fail. So what can you do to reduce your anxiety? This really depends on the sort of person you are, but there are a couple of techniques that we often recommend: rationalizing your thoughts and doing some simple exercises.

Rationalize your thoughts

A good way to take the edge off your anxiety is to think logically about the things that make you anxious. You may, for example, be anxious because you don't know exactly what questions will come up. However, you should bear in mind that you do know that the questions will be structured in a certain way, and if you go through all the practice questions in this book you will have worked with enough examples to have a good idea of what will come up. The wording of the questions will be different, but the underlying logic will be the same, so there's nothing to worry about. You will have practised the thought processes required to solve all the different types of question, and this will make it easy to solve the questions, even if they are worded differently.

Perhaps the root of your worry lies in the idea that you are being judged and that you have to get everything right so you don't come across as stupid. If this is the case, it might help to put things into perspective. Remember that the test will probably be marked by a computer or by a psychometric testing professional who will have seen hundreds, if not thousands, of answer sheets. Your prospective employer will be interested in your overall scores not in whether you get one or two specific questions right or wrong, so you needn't worry about a silly mistake coming back to haunt you.

The major source of concern for most people will be the consequences of the test. What happens if you don't do well enough to get the job? Again, a bit of perspective can help. You might really want the job: it may seem perfect for you or sound like a once-in-a-lifetime opportunity. The truth is, however, that there is no such thing as a perfect job. Every job has its pros and cons, and before you actually start work there is no way of telling if the job will suit you. How can you know if you will get on with your boss or with your new colleagues? Will you be able to handle the workload? And as for once-in-a-lifetime opportunities, who can tell what's round the corner? There may be an even better job on the horizon – you just have to keep looking for it.

You should also bear in mind that if you are not the right person for the job, the job is probably not right for you. It may seem hard to take, but if the recruiters decide not to give you the job, it's probably for good reasons. After all, there is no point wasting your time in a job you won't enjoy and that's hard to handle because it requires different skills from the ones you have. It would be much better to find a job that you'll be good at because you have the right skills and abilities. So, prepare and do your best but remember that this is not the most important moment in your life!

Do relaxation exercises

If rationalizing your anxieties doesn't work for you, it might help to learn a few simple relaxation exercises. There is one called the 'progressive muscular relaxation technique'. Although it has a rather grand name, all you need do is concentrate on one set of muscles at a time – for example, your toes, followed by your feet, followed by your calves and so on – and tense each group of muscles for a few seconds before relaxing them to their original state, and then relaxing them even more until you are as relaxed as possible. Have you ever noticed that when you're a bit stressed your shoulders start to hunch? This can be a really good way of reminding yourself how tense your muscles are and how relaxed they can be.

If you are interested in trying out different relaxation techniques, the easiest way to look for these is on the internet. Search for 'relaxation techniques', choose one and practise it on a few occasions. Once you find one that works for you, you'll be able to do it on testing day.

Even if you manage to rationalize your thoughts and perform some relaxation exercises, you may still feel some anxiety during the testing session. Don't let this alarm you: it's good for you. Research shows that small levels of anxiety actually help your performance. Anxiety keeps you alert and speeds up your mental processing.

The night before

Tiredness

I'm sure people have already advised you many times to get a good night's sleep before you take any exams. The same is true for numerical tests, which are also designed to test your maximum performance. Remember to get a good night's sleep before a numerical test, even if you feel that you need to do some more practice questions.

The benefit you will get from being rested and alert is much greater than the benefit you will get from a few hours of extra practice on the night before your test. Moreover, if you come across an item that you can't solve, this is bound to increase your anxiety. The harm your anxiety will have on your performance is much greater than the benefit you will gain from learning to solve one particular item at this stage.

Mood

You might think that your mood is not important, but many studies have shown that mood affects performance. The rule is simple: being in a good mood can help a person's performance, whereas being in a bad mood can harm their performance. You can, of course, argue that your mood is not something you can alter, so what is the point in mentioning it? Maybe you cannot change your mood, but you can definitely make an effort to avoid circumstances that will get you into a bad mood, such as discussing sensitive subjects on the day of the testing or the night before.

The testing day

If you are invited to complete a numerical test in a testing place rather than completing it online, there are some basic things you should remember.

First of all, make sure that you arrive at the testing place in good time. If you are late, they will not wait for you, and you will miss the test. Even if they do allow you to complete the test at a later date, punctuality is important for every job, so this will give a bad first impression. Ideally, you should aim to arrive at the testing place about 20 minutes before the arranged time. This will allow you to be prepared for unexpected conditions, such as heavy traffic, and will also give you some time to concentrate and relax before the session begins. Remember that you will be dealing with your natural anxiety about the test right before the session, so you should avoid the extra anxiety of whether you will get there on time.

Make sure you have everything you need. Pens, pencils, a calculator, glasses, your hearing aid – write yourself a checklist before the day of the test and stick to it. Also, don't forget to take the invitation letter, your passport or any other documents you have been asked to bring along.

Finally, wear comfortable clothing. You must minimize the things that will distract you during the test, so make sure your clothes are not going to cause you any discomfort.

The testing session

Asking questions

Some people seem to ask questions at every opportunity, but others hate speaking up so much that they'll ask a question only if they absolutely cannot manage without the answer. People who always ask questions are likely to be extroverted and confident, whereas people who tend to be a bit shy might be introverted and self-critical. If you are shy, however, the testing session is one of those situations when you have to get over this. If you have a question, no matter how uncomfortable it might make you feel, you have to ask.

If there is anything you don't understand about the testing procedure or the test instructions or if there's anything you need to change in the testing conditions – for example, if the air conditioning is blowing right at you and you would like to change your seat – talk to the administrator. If you can't find the right time to do so, remember that the administrator will always ask 'Are there any questions?' before the test begins. You should remember that the administrator will not be able to answer any questions about the instructions after the test has started. Make sure you deal with any practical issues, such as changing your seat, before the test has started, otherwise you will lose time and probably your concentration.

During the test

The most important things to do during the test are to stay calm and concentrate. However, you must also consider the following points.

Most tests are in a multiple-choice format, and you will typically fill in your answers on an answer sheet rather than on the actual test. Remember to double-check that your answers correspond to the questions.

You must fill in your answers in the way that you have been instructed. If you have been asked to use a pencil, use a pencil; if you have been asked to put a line in the appropriate circle rather than filling it in, that is what you should do. Computers are often used to score the tests automatically, so you must make sure that the computer will be able to read your answers.

If you cannot decide between two responses, don't choose both. This will be marked as an incorrect response, even if one of your two choices is correct.

If you have no idea how to solve a question or if you find it very difficult or confusing, go on to the next question. Your final score will depend on how many questions you answer not on whether you have missed out a question. However, bear in mind that questions tend to get progressively harder as you go through a test. It's best not to skip questions if you simply think they will take up a lot of time. Do so only if you think you can't solve them.

Guessing the answer

Should you make a guess if you cannot solve a question? Test administrators often get asked this question, and they always answer in one of two ways: 'I'm sorry, I don't have that information' or 'I'm sorry, I can't give you that information'.

Unfortunately, we are in exactly the same position. Sometimes incorrect answers are scored with a negative point, sometimes they are just not scored, so it is impossible to say for certain if it's worth taking a guess if you don't know the answer.

As a rule, if you are not sure about the correct answer, make your best guess but try not to answer entirely at random. For example, if you can rule out three of five available options, you might decide to make an educated guess as to the correct one of the two remaining options. However, it's not a great idea to pick an answer at random if you can't eliminate any of the options.

After the test

After you have completed the test, you will probably want to forget all about it until you receive your results. It is, however, a good idea to try to think about the types of questions you found most difficult and the ones you're most unsure about. We hope that you will have passed on to the next stage in the recruitment process and won't have to sit another test for the time being. However, you never know when you might have to take another one, so it is a good idea to learn as much as you can from the one you've just taken. Numerical tests are being used more and more frequently, and you want to make sure that you are able to complete them to the best of your ability.

Feedback

Typically, a few days after the testing session, you will receive feedback on your results. This could take the form of a simple notice telling you if you have passed on to the next stage of the recruitment process, or it could be a more detailed report, showing, for example, where your score was in relation to the comparison group – that is, what percentage of the comparison group scored lower than you. For example, a more detailed report could look like this:

> You recently completed a numerical ability test. This test is designed to provide a fair, objective, rapid and practical measure of your skills in evaluating numerical information, which are skills that are relevant in many managerial roles.
>
> To give meaning to your scores, they have been compared to a group of other managers. When interpreting the test scores it is important to remember that all scores are relative to this group. Remember also that while numerical ability is important for managers, it is only part of the picture. Many people have useful

strategies to compensate for less well developed skills of numerical analysis. Your score is in the 60th percentile of the comparison group of managers. In other words, you performed at a level that was typical of most people in your comparison group.

If you don't receive any feedback on your test results, our advice is to ask for it. Learning about your abilities will help in your development, irrespective of what happens with the specific job you applied for.

3 Types of questions in numerical tests

Numerical tests are typically found in two basic formats:

- A series of number-based questions and calculations.
- Numerical data shown in a table, graph or a chart, followed by a series of questions on the data; tests like this also assess your ability to extract numerical information presented in various formats.

Companies use numerical tests of both formats in their recruitment process, but the second type is the more common, especially if the tests are for graduate or managerial positions, because the ability to extract numerical information presented in various formats is often required at these levels.

This chapter will take you through both sorts of tests. The practice questions will either include a space for you to write your answer or will give you multiple answers, so that you can choose the one you think is correct. The correct answers are given in the final section of this book.

Simple calculations

All tests will expect you to have a basic knowledge of simple calculations. So we will start from there.

Basic numerical calculations

Adding, subtracting, multiplying and dividing are all basic numerical calculations. It's unlikely that a question will require just these basic calculations, but as they are the cornerstones of a lot of numerical thinking, it's probable that you would need to use these as part of the solution. Usually you will be able to use a calculator during the test, but remember that if you can do simple calculations in your head you will save yourself a lot of valuable time.

Below are a few examples to jog your memory on basic calculations. During the testing session you can perform the ones you are comfortable with in your head and use a calculator only for the ones you are less confident with.

For the practice questions that follow, calculate the value that should replace the x. Remember that time will be important in the actual test, so you should start practising your speed as well as your accuracy.

Practice questions

Try to solve the following examples as quickly as you can.

	QUESTION	ANSWER
1.	$32 + 56 = x$	
2.	$28 + 47 = x$	
3.	$57 + 43 = x$	
4.	$44 + 37 = x$	
5.	$19 + 28 = x$	
6.	$12 + x = 94$	

7. $43 + x = 102$

....

8. $34 + x = 71$

....

9. $x + 6 = 32$

....

10. $x + 28 = 73$

....

11. $23 - 17 = x$

....

12. $97 - 36 = x$

....

13. $45 - 26 = x$

....

14. $87 - 34 = x$

....

15. $39 - 14 = x$

....

16. $3 \times 11 = x$

....

17. $7 \times 8 = x$

....

18. $6 \times 9 = x$

....

19. $5 \times 12 = x$

....

20. $9 \times 5 = x$

....

21. $4 \times x = 48$

....

22. $x \times 5 = 45$

....

23. $x \times 8 = 72$

....

24. $6 \times x = 72$

....

25. $7 \times x = 49$

....

26. $63 \div 9 = x$

....

27. $36 \div 3 = x$

....

28. $56 \div 2 = x$

....

29. $54 \div 6 = x$

....

30. $56 \div 8 = x$

....

Numerical estimation

Another strategy to practise is estimation. It can sometimes be quicker to round off numbers and make a rough calculation in your head than reaching immediately for a calculator. Although this might not give you the exact answer, it might get you close enough to see which of the multiple-choice options is the correct answer. For example, you may have to calculate 51×19, a difficult calculation to do in your head, and your options are: (a) 245 (b) 591 (c) 969 (d) 2115 and (e) 3001. 51 and 19 are close to 50 and 20, so a quick way to solve this question would be to work out 50×20 in your head (1,000), then select the option closest to 1,000, which in this case is 969.

You will have noticed that there are two elements to this question that make it a good candidate for estimation. The first is that 50×20 is an easy calculation and one that most people would feel confident doing in their head. This is an important point to remember, and if at any stage you don't feel confident about the type of calculation you will need to do, it is better to use a calculator. The second element is that the multiple choice options are distant from each other. If you had worked out that the answer to 51×19 was something close to 1,000, but the options were (a) 958 (b) 977 (c) 969 (d) 999 and (e) 1,005 it would be very difficult to make a good estimation and so safer to turn to the calculator.

The practice questions that follow will give you a chance to practise numerical estimations and give you an idea of the types of question it may be suitable to estimate in order to get a quick answer.

Practice questions

....

	QUESTION	ANSWER
31.	$19 \times 21 =$	

    a. 353

    b. 377

    c. 399

    d. 480

    e. 434

....

	QUESTION	ANSWER
32.	$11,489 + 602 =$	

    a. 731

    b. 2,091

    c. 7,491

    d. 12,091

    e. 72,491

....

....

QUESTION   ANSWER

33.   98,765 − 4,321 =

    a. 44,444

    b. 54,444

    c. 55,444

    d. 74,444

    e. 94,444

....

QUESTION   ANSWER

34.   564 ÷ 47 =

    a. 5

    b. 12

    c. 22

    d. 25

    e. 36

....

QUESTION   ANSWER

35.   1,015 ÷ 5 =

    a. 27

    b. 51

    c. 203

    d. 550

    e. 840

....

| QUESTION | ANSWER |

36. $299 \times 31 =$

    a. 393
    b. 754
    c. 3,269
    d. 9,269
    e. 16,058

| QUESTION | ANSWER |

37. $135,213 - 45,682 =$

    a. 89,531
    b. 100,048
    c. 110,354
    d. 120,597
    e. 130,597

| QUESTION | ANSWER |

38. $22,133 + 48,572 =$

    a. 25,491
    b. 60,484
    c. 64,525
    d. 70,705
    e. 87,641

QUESTION	ANSWER

39. $498 \times 61 =$

   a. 20,946
   b. 30,378
   c. 36,516
   d. 40,922
   e. 44,922

QUESTION	ANSWER

40. $42,521 \div 421 =$

   a. 10
   b. 12
   c. 23
   d. 48
   e. 101

QUESTION	ANSWER

41. $798 + 597 =$

   a. 855
   b. 1,005
   c. 1,395
   d. 1,804
   e. 2,354

| QUESTION | ANSWER |

42. $149 \times 101 =$

    a. 1,049
    b. 1,549
    c. 10,049
    d. 15,049
    e. 150,049

| QUESTION | ANSWER |

43. $56,648 - 22,473 =$

    a. 1,825
    b. 34,175
    c. 45,570
    d. 53,850
    e. 85,121

| QUESTION | ANSWER |

44. $957 \div 29 =$

    a. 33
    b. 59
    c. 67
    d. 71
    e. 75

QUESTION	ANSWER

45. $610 \div 5 =$

a. 66
b. 122
c. 240
d. 280
e. 307

QUESTION	ANSWER

46. $76,914 - 75,482 =$

a. 154
b. 384
c. 1,432
d. 2,548
e. 3,249

QUESTION	ANSWER

47. $990 \times 20 =$

a. 19,800
b. 28,900
c. 34,800
d. 36,500
e. 48,800

QUESTION	ANSWER

48. $45,679 + 3,215 =$

a. 42,769
b. 45,818
c. 46,987
d. 47,894
e. 48,894

QUESTION	ANSWER

49. $87,636 - 7,777 =$

a. 9,859
b. 16,487
c. 66,429
d. 71,771
e. 79,859

QUESTION	ANSWER

50. $645 \times 49 \times 0 =$

a. 0
b. 1,229
c. 2,594
d. 3,215
e. 31,801

Rounding off answers

Often a numerical question will ask you to round off your answer. You might find it useful to practise with a few examples of rounding off numbers, just to jog your memory, especially if you haven't worked with numbers for some time.

When to round up

Rounding up means that you increase the required digit by a value of 1 and drop off the digits to its right. You need to round up if the number next to the required digit is 5, 6, 7, 8 or 9. For example, if you are required to round off 3.257 to two decimal places, you should round this up, so it becomes 3.26.

When to round down

Rounding down means that you keep the required digit as it is and drop off the digits to its right. You need to round down if the number next to the required digit is 0, 1, 2, 3 or 4. For example, if you are required to round off 0.24 to one decimal place, you should round this down, so it becomes 0.2.

TIP: When you round off to a decimal that has more than one digit on its right, you should consider only the first digit that is on its right. For example, if you are required to round off 0.2349 to two decimal places it should become 0.23. If, on the other hand, you are required to round it off to three decimal places it will become 0.235.

Practice questions

Round off the following numbers to two decimal places.

	QUESTION	ANSWER
51.	68.436	
52.	8.244	
53.	0.6238	
54.	0.7364	
55.	5.289	

Round off the following numbers to one decimal place.

	QUESTION	ANSWER
56.	14.834	
57.	7.162	
58.	3.049	
59.	4.29	
60.	6.368	

Further numerical calculations

The basic numerical calculations are useful because they will help you get to a solution faster, even though they are unlikely to be the main focus of a question. But what types of questions are you likely to have to solve for a numerical test? The most common types of question in numerical tests involve averages, percentages, inverse percentages and ratios. We will, therefore, go through the solution of these questions step by step so that you can see how to solve them quickly and accurately.

These calculations are not only likely to be part of a question but in some cases make up a whole question in themselves. We will go through each category at a time and for each type of question we will give the general solution and also the general formula. Some people find it easier to read a solution as text, while others find it easier to see it as a formula, so if you find that you prefer one of these methods you could focus on that one.

After seeing the general solution, you will also see a solution for a specific example question so that you can double-check your understanding of each type of calculation. You will then be presented with a number of practice questions.

Averages

The average, or mean, of a number of values is simply the sum of the values divided by the number of values. Questions on averages can take several forms, and we will go through them one at a time.

GENERAL QUESTION: What is the average of A, B and C?

GENERAL SOLUTION: Add the values together and divide their total by the number of values.

FORMULA: $(A + B + C) \div Number\ of\ values$

EXAMPLE QUESTION: What is the average of 7, 3, 12 and 26?

SOLUTION: $(7 + 3 + 12 + 26) \div 4 = 48 \div 4 = 12$, so the average of these numbers is 12.

Practice questions

Try the following practice questions on averages, rounding off your answers as required.

QUESTION	ANSWER

61. What is the average of 7, 9, 11 and 6?

    a. 8.25

    b. 8.55

    c. 8.65

    d. 8.75

    e. 8.95

QUESTION	ANSWER

62. What is the average of 130, 315 and 425?

    a. 275

    b. 285

    c. 290

    d. 305

    e. 310

QUESTION   ANSWER

63. What is the average of 1.5, 7.6, 2.4 and 3?

    a. 3.37

    a. 3.42

    c. 3.48

    d. 3.59

    e. 3.63

QUESTION   ANSWER

64. What is the average of 55, 57.5, 59.5, 60 and 61.5?

    a. 56.8

    b. 57.5

    c. 57.9

    d. 58.7

    e. 60.2

QUESTION   ANSWER

65. What is the average of $1/5$, $1/6$ and $1/7$?

    a. 0.15

    b. 0.17

    c. 0.22

    d. 0.25

    e. 0.29

| QUESTION | ANSWER |

66. What is the average of 0.6, 0.2, 0.7 and 0.7?

    a. 0.51
    b. 0.55
    c. 0.58
    d. 0.61
    e. 0.62

In a similar type of question, you could be given the average and all but one of the values and asked to calculate the missing value.

GENERAL QUESTION: What is the value of a, if the average of a, b, c and d is x?

GENERAL SOLUTION: Multiply the average, x, by the number of values that make up the average (here the number of values is 4 because you have a, b, c and d). From this subtract the values that are given (b, c and d). The remaining value is the value of a.

FORMULA: $(x \times \text{Number of values}) - b - c - d$

EXAMPLE QUESTION: If the average of a, 12, 15, 10 and 30 is 15, what is the value of a?

SOLUTION: You have to work out $(15 \times 5) - 12 - 15 - 10 - 30 = 75 - 12 - 15 - 10 - 30 = 8$, so the value of a is 8.

Practice questions

Try the following questions, rounding off your answers as required.

....

| QUESTION | ANSWER |

67. What is the value of A, if the average of A, 100, 150 and 100 is 130?

a. 130
b. 140
c. 150
d. 160
e. 170

....

| QUESTION | ANSWER |

68. What is the value of A, if the average of A, 5 and 20 is 15?

a. 17
b. 18
c. 19
d. 20
e. 21

....

| QUESTION | ANSWER |

69. What is the value of A, if the average of A, 2.5, 3 and 5 is 4?

a. 4.9
b. 5.2
c. 5.5
d. 5.7
e. 5.9

....

QUESTION	ANSWER

70. What is the value of A, if the average of A, 14.25 and 18.5 is 15.6?

   a. 14.05

   b. 14.36

   c. 14.70

   d. 15.12

   e. 15.08

QUESTION	ANSWER

71. What is the value of A, if the average of 14, 20, 22 and A is 24?

   a. 26

   b. 28

   c. 32

   d. 36

   e. 40

QUESTION	ANSWER

72. What is the value of A, if the average of 16, A, 18, 22 and 20 is 16?

   a. 4

   b. 7

   c. 9

   d. 12

   e. 14

The questions you have just worked through were given to help you practise with the calculations involved with averages. In the questions that follow you will see how these calculations can be required within an actual question in a numerical test.

Sample questions

....

QUESTION   ANSWER

73. What was the average temperature in °C this
autumn if the average monthly temperature was
16°C in September, 12°C in October and 8°C in
November?

   a. 10°C

   b. 11°C

   c. 12°C

   d. 13°C

   e. 14°C

....

QUESTION   ANSWER

74. What was the average level of sunlight from
January to June if the monthly levels of sunlight
were 1, 2, 4, 6, 6 and 7?

   a. 4.16

   b. 4.33

   c. 4.67

   d. 5.16

   e. 5.33

....

QUESTION   ANSWER

75. What is the average height of a group of people if the
heights of the group members are 1.85 metres, 1.59
metres, 1.72 metres, 1.64 metres and 1.90 metres?

   a. 1.69 m

   b. 1.71 m

   c. 1.74 m

   d. 1.75 m

   e. 1.79 m

....

QUESTION   ANSWER

76. If five pieces of cheese each weigh 145 g, 155 g,
139 g, 162 g and 159 g what is their average weight?

   a. 146 g
   b. 148 g
   c. 150 g
   d. 152 g
   e. 155 g

QUESTION   ANSWER

77. If a restaurant billed four dinner tables at £50, £80,
£115 and £125, how much was the bill of a dinner
table on average?

   a. £82.50
   b. £84.25
   c. £88.75
   d. £92.50
   e. £94.25

QUESTION   ANSWER

78. If the average 200 metres running time of five
runners was 27.8 seconds, and the timings of four
of the runners were 23.5, 25.1, 29.8 and 30.2
seconds, what was the timing of the fifth runner?

   a. 26.4 sec
   b. 27.6 sec
   c. 28.8 sec
   d. 29.6 sec
   e. 30.4 sec

Percentages

A percentage is a way of expressing a number as a fraction of 100 – in other words, it is a number divided by 100. Therefore, 5 per cent is the same as $5 \div 100$, and it is also the same as 0.05. You should try to become familiar with these transformations, because you will often need to transform a percentage, such as 10 per cent, into a decimal, 0.1, in order to make the calculations required for a numerical reasoning question, and you will often be required to transform the answer back into a percentage. The following examples will help you practise these transformations and also to practise further with rounding off decimals.

Practice questions

Transform the following numbers into percentages, rounding off to one decimal place.

	QUESTION	ANSWER
79.	0.331	
80.	10.350	
81.	0.009	
82.	0.1274	
83.	120.549	

Transform the following percentages into decimals, rounding off your answer to two decimal places.

	QUESTION	ANSWER
84.	26%	
85.	13.2%	
86.	88.6%	
87.	220.3%	
88.	130%	

Transform the following percentages into decimals, rounding off to three decimal places.

	QUESTION	ANSWER
89.	15.68%	
90.	14.7%	
91.	24.33%	
92.	55.55%	
93.	102.78%	

There are many types of questions involving percentages that you could come across in a numerical test. We will go through these in detail in the following pages. Each type of question requires a different calculation, and when you are completing the test, you must concentrate carefully when reading the question, so that you can immediately understand which type of calculation is required.

GENERAL QUESTION: What is x% of A?
GENERAL SOLUTION: Divide *x* by 100 and multiply this by A.
FORMULA: $A \times (x \div 100)$

EXAMPLE QUESTION: What is 15% of 60?
EXAMPLE ANSWER: You have to work out $60 \times (15 \div 100) =$
$60 \times 0.15 = 9$, so the answer is 9.

Note that in order to make the calculations required, you had to transform the percentage, 15 per cent, into a decimal, 0.15. Having solved the transformation practice questions that were presented earlier, you should be able to make this transformation without using a calculator. This will save you time during the test.

Practice questions

Try to solve the following examples as quickly as possible, using a calculator for the calculations, but not for transforming the percentages into decimals. Round off your answers to whole numbers.

QUESTION		ANSWER
94.	What is 40% of 500?	
	a. 180	
	b. 200	
	c. 210	
	d. 220	
	e. 240	

QUESTION	ANSWER

95. What is 16% of 220?

a. 35
b. 38
c. 42
d. 45
e. 48

QUESTION	ANSWER

96. What is 18% of 1,500?

a. 230
b. 250
c. 270
d. 290
e. 310

QUESTION	ANSWER

97. What is 15.5% of 2,000?

a. 295
b. 302
c. 306
d. 310
e. 318

QUESTION	ANSWER

98. What is 0.5% of 400?

a. 1
b. 2
c. 3
d. 4
e. 5

QUESTION   ANSWER

99. What is 120% of 300?

    a. 320

    b. 330

    c. 340

    d. 350

    e. 360

Now that you know how to work out this type of percentage calculation, all you need to do is recognize it when it is required by a question. Look at the questions that follow. They all involve different things, but essentially all they require is for you to find a specific percentage of a given value.

Sample questions

QUESTION   ANSWER

100. If there is a 45% discount on a £15 shirt how much money would you save on this purchase?

    a. £6.75

    b. £7.15

    c. £7.25

    d. £7.50

    e. £7.75

QUESTION   ANSWER

101. If 20 people, of whom 30% were women, attended
a presentation how many women attended the
presentation?

    a. 4
    b. 5
    c. 6
    d. 7
    e. 8

QUESTION   ANSWER

102. If your bonus is 2% of your target and your target
is £5,000,000, how much will your bonus be if you
make your target?

    a. £90,000
    b. £100,000
    c. £150,000
    d. £200,000
    e. £250,000

QUESTION   ANSWER

103. If a 300-hour light bulb worked for only 85% of
its 'life', how many hours did it work for?

    a. 230
    b. 245
    c. 255
    d. 260
    e. 285

QUESTION: What is *x* as a percentage of A?

SOLUTION: Divide *x* by A and transform this into a percentage.

FORMULA: $(x \div A) \times 100\%$

EXAMPLE QUESTION: What is 10 as a percentage of 40?

EXAMPLE ANSWER: You have to work out $10 \div 40$. This will give you 0.25, which you have to transform into a percentage, so the answer is 25%.

Practice questions

QUESTION	ANSWER

104. What is 4 as a percentage of 24?

   a. 15%

   b. 17%

   c. 19%

   d. 22%

   e. 25%

QUESTION	ANSWER

105. What is 30 as a percentage of 270?

   a. 11%

   b. 14%

   c. 17%

   d. 20%

   e. 22%

QUESTION	ANSWER

106. What is 12 as a percentage of 300?

    a. 4%
    b. 8%
    c. 10%
    d. 12%
    e. 14%

QUESTION	ANSWER

107. What is 45 as a percentage of 200?

    a. 15%
    b. 17%
    c. 21%
    d. 23%
    e. 25%

QUESTION	ANSWER

108. What is 150 as a percentage of 600?

    a. 17%
    b. 19%
    c. 21%
    d. 23%
    e. 25%

109. What is 250 as a percentage of 200?

    a. 105%

    b. 110%

    c. 120%

    d. 125%

    e. 130%

Sample questions

For the following questions, round off your answers to integers – that is, to whole numbers.

110. What percentage of the total sales were due to desktops if total sales were £1,200,000 and sales due to desktops were £460,000?

    a. 38%

    b. 40%

    c. 42%

    d. 44%

    e. 46%

111. What percentage of your revenue was due to your bonus if your total revenue was £80,000 and your bonus was £35,000?

    a. 38%

    b. 40%

    c. 42%

    d. 44%

    e. 46%

| QUESTION | ANSWER |

112. What percentage of water consumption was due to the washing machine if water consumption was 80,000 litres and consumption due to the washing machine was 10,500 litres?

    a. 10%

    b. 13%

    c. 15%

    d. 16%

    e. 18%

| QUESTION | ANSWER |

113. What percentage of the floor is covered by the carpet if the floor is 90 m² and the carpet is 50 m²?

    a. 48%

    b. 50%

    c. 52%

    d. 55%

    e. 56%

QUESTION: What is A increased by x%?

SOLUTION: Add x to 100. Divide this by 100 and then multiply it by A.

FORMULA: $A \times [(100 + x) \div 100]$

EXAMPLE QUESTION: What is 20 increased by 2%?

EXAMPLE ANSWER: You have to work out $20 \times [(100 + 2) \div 100]$
$= 20 \times (102 \div 100) = 20 \times 1.02$, so the answer is 20.4.

TIP: When you have to work out this type of question, there is a short-cut that you can use rather than going through all these calculations. Transform x into decimals and add 1. This has the same value as $[(100 + x) \div 100]$. So if you multiply this directly by A, you will get your answer. In the example presented, if you transform 2 per cent into 0.02 and add 1, this will give you 1.02. Now multiply this by 20 and you have your answer. As you can see, this just takes you directly to the final calculation, skipping the first two steps and saving you time. Try to solve the following questions by using this shortcut.

Practice questions

QUESTION	ANSWER

114. What is 400 increased by 15%?

    a. 445

    b. 450

    c. 460

    d. 465

    e. 475

QUESTION	ANSWER

115. What is 15 increased by 60%?

    a. 21

    b. 24

    c. 26

    d. 29

    e. 31

QUESTION   **ANSWER**

116. What is 110 increased by 10%?

    a. 115
    b. 117
    c. 119
    d. 121
    e. 123

QUESTION   **ANSWER**

117. What is 0.5 increased by 25%?

    a. 0.57
    b. 0.61
    c. 0.63
    d. 0.65
    e. 0.68

QUESTION   **ANSWER**

118. What is 1,000,000 increased by 0.5%?

    a. 1,005,000
    b. 1,010,000
    c. 1,015,000
    d. 1,020,000
    e. 1,025,000

QUESTION	ANSWER

119. What is 200 increased by 110%?

    a. 405
    b. 410
    c. 415
    d. 420
    e. 425

TIP: Do not get confused when the question is about an increase that is over 100 per cent. For example, in Question 119 you had to calculate 200 increased by 110 per cent. By following all the steps of the solution you would work out $200 \times [(110 + 100) \div 100] = 200 \times (210 \div 100)) = 200 \times 2.10$. Or, by using the shortcut, this would be $200 \times (1.1 + 1) = 200 \times 2.1$. A common mistake here would be to multiply 200 by just 1.1. This would give you an increase of 10 per cent rather than 110 per cent, which would be wrong.

Sample questions

QUESTION	ANSWER

120. If the temperature is 20°C and rises by 15%, what will it become?

    a. 21°C
    b. 22°C
    c. 23°C
    d. 24°C
    e. 25°C

QUESTION   ANSWER

121. What will John's height be if it is currently 1.60
metres and it increases by 15%?

    a. 1.70 m

    b. 1.74 m

    c. 1.78 m

    d. 1.80 m

    e. 1.84 m

QUESTION   ANSWER

122. If the production of light bulbs increases from 6
million parts by 2%, how many parts will be
produced?

    a. 6,100,000

    b. 6,120,000

    c. 6,180,000

    d. 6,200,000

    e. 6,240,000

QUESTION   ANSWER

123. What will Collin's salary be if he gets a 10% raise
on his current £35,000 a year?

    a. £36,000

    b. £37,500

    c. £38,000

    d. £38,500

    e. £39,000

TIP: A trickier variation of this question is when you are asked about a successive percentage increase. Look for example at the following question.

....

QUESTION   ANSWER

124. If a company's revenue increases from £20,000,000
     by 10% per year, what will it be in 3 years?

     a. £22,000,000
     b. £24,200,000
     c. £26,000,000
     d. £26,620,000
     e. £26,800,000

....

To solve this question, you need to calculate the percentage increase successively for each year. So you need to work out:

In 1 year: 20,000,000 × 1.10 = 22,000,000
In 2 years: 22,000,000 × 1.10 = 24,200,000
In 3 years: 24,200,000 × 1.10 = 26,620,000

So the answer is £26,620,000. This is not, in fact, a more difficult question, it just requires you to make the same calculations more than once.

QUESTION: What is A decreased by x%?
SOLUTION: Subtract x from 100. Divide this value by 100 and multiply by A.
FORMULA: $A \times [(100 - x) \div 100)]$

EXAMPLE QUESTION: What is 60 decreased by 10%?
EXAMPLE ANSWER: You have to work out $60 \times [(100 - 10) \div 100]$
$= 60 \times (90 \div 100) = 60 \times 0.9$, so the answer is 54.

TIP: As with the increase in percentages, there is also a shortcut with the decrease in percentages. You should again transform x per cent into decimals, and this time subtract this from 1. Multiply this value by A to get to the answer directly. In the example above, if you transform 10 per cent to 0.1 and subtract this from 1, you will get 0.9. Multiply this by 60 and you are again at the final calculation that gives you the answer. This method is faster, but it requires you to work out $1 - 0.1$ mentally. This is an example of when the simple calculations, which were given in the beginning of this section, come in handy.

Practice questions

QUESTION   ANSWER

125. What is 50 decreased by 25%?

   a. 30.0
   b. 32.5
   c. 35.0
   d. 37.5
   e. 39.0

QUESTION   ANSWER

126. What is 300 decreased by 15%?

   a. 245
   b. 250
   c. 255
   d. 260
   e. 265

QUESTION   ANSWER

127. What is 1,500 decreased by 3%?

   a. 1,455
   b. 1,460
   c. 1,465
   d. 1,470
   e. 1,475

QUESTION   ANSWER

128. What is 725 decreased by 40%?

   a. 430
   b. 435
   c. 440
   d. 445
   e. 450

QUESTION	ANSWER

129. What is 0.60 decreased by 20%?

   a. 0.40
   b. 0.42
   c. 0.45
   d. 0.48
   e. 0.50

QUESTION	ANSWER

130. What is 1,500,000 decreased by 0.5%?

   a. 1,490,000
   b. 1,492,500
   c. 1,495,500
   d. 1,497,000
   e. 1,499,500

Sample questions

QUESTION	ANSWER

131. How many employees will a company have if 15%
   of its 80 employees are made redundant?

   a. 65
   b. 66
   c. 68
   d. 70
   e. 72

QUESTION   ANSWER

132. How much would you pay for a jacket if its
original price is £120 and it has a 40% reduction
due to sales?

    a. £60
    b. £65
    c. £70
    d. £72
    e. £76

QUESTION   ANSWER

133. How many words will an assignment have, if its
6,000 words should be reduced by 10%?

    a. 5,400
    b. 5,500
    c. 5,600
    d. 5,700
    e. 5,800

QUESTION   ANSWER

134. How many cows are healthy if 6% of the 300 cows
are sick?

    a. 280
    b. 282
    c. 284
    d. 286
    e. 288

QUESTION: What is the percentage increase from A to B?

SOLUTION: Divide B by A and subtract 1 from the value you obtain. Then transform this into a percentage.

FORMULA: $[(B \div A) - 1] \times 100\%$

EXAMPLE QUESTION: What is the percentage increase from 20 to 20.4?

EXAMPLE ANSWER: You have to work out $(20.4 \div 20) - 1 = 1.02 - 1 = 0.02$. Transform this back to a percentage, so the answer is 2%.

Note that this requires the opposite calculation to the question asking 'What is 20 increased by 2%?' Remember that for that question the solution required you to add 0.02 to 1 (this was explained in the tip), which is 1.02, and to multiply this by 20, yielding 20.4.

TIP: Again, do not get confused when the increase is over 100 per cent. For example, if you have to calculate the percentage increase from 10 to 30, you have to work out $(30 \div 10) - 1 = 3 - 1 = 2$. Transform this to a percentage, so the answer is 200 per cent. A common mistake here would be to calculate $30 \div 10$, which is 3, and then forget to subtract 1 out of this. This would make you answer that the increase was 300 per cent. However, 10 increased by 300 per cent is actually 40 and not 30.

Practice questions

Solve the following practice questions, rounding off your answers to whole numbers.

....

QUESTION   ANSWER

135. What is the percentage increase from 12 to 18?

    a. 40%
    b. 45%
    c. 50%
    d. 55%
    e. 60%

....

QUESTION   ANSWER

136. What is the percentage increase from 300 to 650?

    a. 110%
    b. 112%
    c. 115%
    d. 117%
    e. 120%

....

QUESTION   ANSWER

137. What is the percentage increase from 1,200,000 to 1,600,000?

    a. 33%
    b. 35%
    c. 37%
    d. 38%
    e. 40%

....

QUESTION	ANSWER

138. What is the percentage increase from 0.75 to 1.25?

    a. 59%
    b. 61%
    c. 63%
    d. 65%
    e. 67%

QUESTION	ANSWER

139. What is the percentage increase from 8 to 40?

    a. 300%
    b. 350%
    c. 380%
    d. 400%
    e. 420%

QUESTION	ANSWER

140. What is the percentage increase from 100 to 400?

    a. 280%
    b. 300%
    c. 310%
    d. 315%
    e. 330%

Sample questions

....

QUESTION   ANSWER

141. What is the percentage increase in your hard drive
if you revert from a 40G hard drive to a 100G hard
drive?

    a. 120%

    b. 130%

    c. 140%

    d. 150%

    e. 160%

....

QUESTION   ANSWER

142. What is the percentage increase of your rent if it
increases from £600 a month to £650 a month?

    a. 4%

    b. 5%

    c. 6%

    d. 7%

    e. 8%

....

QUESTION   ANSWER

143. What is the percentage increase of the time you
have to complete an 18-minute test if you are
allowed 20 minutes to complete it?

    a. 9%

    b. 10%

    c. 11%

    d. 12%

    e. 13%

....

QUESTION	ANSWER

144. What is the percentage increase of your monthly savings if they go from £400 to £460?

    a. 12%

    b. 15%

    c. 18%

    d. 20%

    e. 22%

QUESTION: What is the percentage decrease from B to A?

SOLUTION: Subtract A from B and divide this by B. Transform this into a percentage.

FORMULA: $[(B - A) \div B] \times 100\%$

EXAMPLE QUESTION: What is the percentage decrease from 80 to 60?

EXAMPLE ANSWER: You have to work out $[(80 - 60) \div 80] = 20 \div 80 = 0.25$. Transform this back into a percentage, so the answer is 25 per cent.

TIP: When you are performing this type of calculation, try to subtract A from B in your head to save time.

Practice questions

....

QUESTION   ANSWER

145. What is the percentage decrease from 12 to 8?

    a. 31%

    b. 33%

    c. 35%

    d. 37%

    e. 39%

....

QUESTION   ANSWER

146. What is the percentage decrease from 85 to 60?

    a. 29%

    b. 30%

    c. 31%

    d. 32%

    e. 33%

....

QUESTION   ANSWER

147. What is the percentage decrease from 65 to 20?

    a. 55%

    b. 61%

    c. 69%

    d. 72%

    e. 75%

....

QUESTION	ANSWER

148. What is the percentage decrease from 1.25 to 0.25?

    a. 65%

    b. 70%

    c. 75%

    d. 80%

    e. 85%

QUESTION	ANSWER

149. What is the percentage decrease from 1,800 to 1,400?

    a. 15%

    b. 16%

    c. 18%

    d. 20%

    e. 22%

QUESTION	ANSWER

150. What is the percentage decrease from 175 to 26?

    a. 70%

    b. 75%

    c. 80%

    d. 85%

    e. 90%

Sample questions

....

QUESTION	ANSWER

151. By what percentage would someone's weight decrease if they went from 88 kg to 83 kg?

    a. 5.02%

    b. 5.24%

    c. 5.46%

    d. 5.68%

    e. 5.80%

....

QUESTION	ANSWER

152. The safety height on a ride at a theme park is reduced from 1.64 metres to 1.52 metres. What is the percentage decrease in the safety height?

    a. 7.1%

    b. 7.2%

    c. 7.3%

    d. 7.4%

    e. 7.5%

....

QUESTION	ANSWER

153. What is the percentage decrease in the time you work if you go from an 8 hour day to a 7.5 hour day?

    a. 6.25%

    b. 6.26%

    c. 6.27%

    d. 6.28%

    e. 6.29%

....

QUESTION   ANSWER

154. What is the percentage decrease of a 25,000 m^2
forest, if 20,000 m^2 of the forest survives from a
fire?

    a. 20%

    b. 35%

    c. 50%

    d. 65%

    e. 80%

Ratios

Ratios are used to make comparisons between two things. The most common way to present ratios is by writing 'the ratio of A to B' or by writing 'A:B'. Note that if the ratio of A to B is 3:1, this simply means that A is 3 times greater than B. As with percentages, there are various types of questions that can involve ratios. These are described in the pages that follow.

QUESTION: What is the ratio of A to B, if A = a and B = b?
SOLUTION: Divide a by b. This quotient to 1 is the ratio of a to b.
FORMULA: $a \div b : 1$

EXAMPLE QUESTION: What is the ratio of A to B, if A = 12 and B = 16?
EXAMPLE ANSWER: The ratio of A to B is 12 ÷ 16:1 = 0.75:1

Practice questions

QUESTION	ANSWER

155. What is the ratio of A:B, if A = 800 and B = 200?

    a. 3.5:1
    b. 3.8:1
    c. 4.0:1
    d. 4.2:1
    e. 4.5:1

QUESTION	ANSWER

156. What is the ratio of A:B, if A = 0.3 and B = 0.6?

    a. 0.4:1
    b. 0.5:1
    c. 0.6:1
    d. 0.7:1
    e. 0.8:1

QUESTION	ANSWER

157. What is the ratio of A:B, if A = 500 and B = 200?

    a. 1.5:1
    b. 2.0:1
    c. 2.2:1
    d. 2.5:1
    e. 3.0:1

QUESTION	ANSWER

158. What is the ratio of A:B, if A = 90 and B = 15?

    a. 4.0:1
    b. 4.5:1
    c. 5.0:1
    d. 5.5:1
    e. 6.0:1

QUESTION   ANSWER

159. What is the ratio of A:B, if A = 24 and B = 18?

    a. 1.33:1
    b. 1.35:1
    c. 1.37:1
    d. 1.39:1
    e. 1.41:1

QUESTION   ANSWER

160. What is the ratio of A:B, if A = 34 and B = 59.5?

    a. 0.55:1
    b. 0.57:1
    c. 0.59:1
    d. 0.61:1
    e. 0.63:1

Sample questions

QUESTION   ANSWER

161. What is the ratio of children to adults in a group if there are 70 children and 45 adults in the group?

    a. 1.56
    b. 1.66
    c. 1.77
    d. 1.88
    e. 1.99

QUESTION   **ANSWER**

162. What is the ratio of cordial to water in a drink, if
there are 125 ml of cordial and 500 ml of water in
the drink?

    a. 0.20:1
    b. 0.25:1
    c. 0.30:1
    d. 0.35:1
    e. 0.40:1

QUESTION   **ANSWER**

163. What is the ratio of examples to test questions if
there are 5 examples and 35 test questions?

    a. 0.10:1
    b. 0.11:1
    c. 0.12:1
    d. 0.13:1
    e. 0.14:1

QUESTION   **ANSWER**

164. What is the ratio of Julie's age to Anna's age if Julie
is 30 and Anna is 21?

    a. 1.40:1
    b. 1.41:1
    c. 1.42:1
    d. 1.43:1
    e. 1.44:1

Another type of question that you can come across involving ratios, is when you are given the ratio of two groups and the size of one of the two groups, and you are asked to calculate the size of the second group.

QUESTION: If the ratio of A to B is $x{:}y$ and B = b, what is the size of A?
SOLUTION: Divide x by y and multiply this quotient by b.
FORMULA: $b \times (x \div y)$

EXAMPLE QUESTION: If the ratio of pens to pencils is 5:2, and there are 16 pencils, how many pens are there?
EXAMPLE SOLUTION: You have to work out $16 \times (5 \div 2) = 16 \times 2.5 = 40$.

Similarly, you may be given the value of A and asked to work out the value of B.

QUESTION: If the ratio of A to B is $x{:}y$, and A = a, what is the size of B?
SOLUTION: Divide y by x and multiply this quotient by a.
FORMULA: $a \times (y \div x)$

EXAMPLE QUESTION: If the ratio of pens to pencils is 5:1 and there are 50 pens, how many pencils are there?
EXAMPLE SOLUTION: You have to work out $50 \times (1 \div 5) = 50 \times 0.2 = 10$.

Practice questions

QUESTION   ANSWER

165. If the ratio of A to B is 3:1 and B = 17, what is the size of A?

    a. 51

    b. 52

    c. 53

    d. 54

    e. 55

QUESTION   ANSWER

166. If the ratio of A to B is 2:3, and B = 75, what is the size of A?

    a. 35

    b. 45

    c. 50

    d. 55

    e. 60

QUESTION   ANSWER

167. If the ratio of A to B is 4:5, and B is 250, what is the size of A?

    a. 180

    b. 200

    c. 215

    d. 220

    e. 225

QUESTION   ANSWER

168. If the ratio of A to B is 7.5:1, and A is 75, what is
the size of B?

a. 5
b. 10
c. 15
d. 20
e. 25

QUESTION   ANSWER

169. If the ratio of A to B is 1:6, and A is 2.5, what is the
size of B?

a. 8
b. 10
c. 12
d. 15
e. 20

QUESTION   ANSWER

170. If the ratio of A to B is 3:7, and A is 27, what is the
size of B?

a. 49
b. 50
c. 56
d. 60
e. 63

Sample questions

....

QUESTION   **ANSWER**

171. If the ratio of cola to lemonade cans in a fridge
before a party is 4:3 and there are 48 cans of
lemonade, how many cans of cola are there?

    a. 60
    b. 62
    c. 64
    d. 66
    e. 68

....

QUESTION   **ANSWER**

172. If the ratio of magazines to newspapers in a shop
is 8:3 and there are 60 newspapers, how many
magazines are there?

    a. 120
    b. 130
    c. 140
    d. 150
    e. 160

....

QUESTION   **ANSWER**

173. If the ratio of red tablecloths to green tablecloths in a restaurant is 6:5 and there are 15 green tablecloths, how many red tablecloths are there?

    a. 16
    b. 17
    c. 18
    d. 19
    e. 20

QUESTION   **ANSWER**

174. If the ratio of males to females in an office is 1.4:1 and there are 30 females, how many males are there?

    a. 40
    b. 42
    c. 44
    d. 46
    e. 48

Another type of question that you could be asked on ratios is when you are given the total number of a group and the ratio of its subgroups, and you are asked to find the size of the subgroups.

QUESTION: If A consists of B and C, and the ratio of B to C is x:y, what is the size of B?

SOLUTION: Divide x by the sum of x and y. Multiply this quotient by A.

FORMULA: $A \times [x \div (x + y)]$

EXAMPLE QUESTION: If there are 180 people in a cinema with a male to female ratio of 3:1, how many males are in the cinema?

EXAMPLE ANSWER: You have to work out $180 \times [3 \div (3+1)] = 180 \times 3 \div 4 = 135$.

Similarly, you could be given the value of B and asked for the value of C. The question then would be:

QUESTION: If A consists of B and C, and the ratio of B to C is x:y, what is the size of C?

SOLUTION: Divide y by the sum of x and y. Multiply this quotient by A.

FORMULA: $A \times [y \div (x + y)]$

EXAMPLE QUESTION: If there are 60 animals on a farm with a sheep to chicken ratio of 5:1, how many chickens are on the farm?

EXAMPLE ANSWER: You have to work out $60 \times [1 \div (5+1)] = 60 \times 1 \div 6 = 10$.

Practice questions

Work out the following examples, for a total, A, of 300.

QUESTION	ANSWER

175. What is the size of B, if the ratio of B to C is 1:5?

    a. 40

    b. 45

    c. 50

    d. 55

    e. 60

QUESTION	ANSWER

176. What is the size of C, if the ratio of B to C is 1:7?

    a. 262.0

    b. 262.5

    c. 265.0

    d. 265.5

    e. 270.0

QUESTION	ANSWER

177. What is the size of B, if the ratio of B to C is 0.25:1?

    a. 60

    b. 80

    c. 100

    d. 120

    e. 240

| QUESTION | ANSWER |

178. What is the size of B, if the ratio of B to C is 1.5:1?

    a. 165

    b. 170

    c. 175

    d. 180

    e. 185

| QUESTION | ANSWER |

179. What is the size of C, if the ratio of B to C is 1:1.25?

    a. 166.67

    b. 172.33

    c. 175.27

    d. 176.46

    e. 180.15

| QUESTION | ANSWER |

180. What is the size of B, if the ratio of B to C is 5:3?

    a. 182.0

    b. 185.3

    c. 187.5

    d. 188.6

    e. 190.5

Sample questions

Work out the following examples, given that the total population of Edinburgh is 450,000. Round off your answers to whole numbers.

QUESTION   ANSWER

181. How many women are there in Edinburgh if the
male to female ratio is 0.98:1?

    a. 227,270
    b. 227,271
    c. 227,272
    d. 227,273
    e. 227,274

QUESTION   ANSWER

182. If the ratio of people employed to those not in
employment in Edinburgh is 1.04:1, how many
people are employed?

    a. 229,410
    b. 229,411
    c. 229,412
    d. 229,413
    e. 229,414

QUESTION   ANSWER

183. How many people are over 15 in Edinburgh if the
      ratio of people aged 15 or less to people aged over
      15 is 1:6.2?

      a. 387,500
      b. 387,501
      c. 387,502
      d. 387,503
      e. 387,504

QUESTION   ANSWER

184. How many people are under 65 in Edinburgh if
      the ratio of people aged less than 65 to people
      aged 65 or more is 8:1?

      a. 400,000
      b. 400,010
      c. 400,020
      d. 400,030
      e. 400,040

Ways of presenting numerical data

Numerical reasoning questions can include the numerical data within the questions themselves or the data can be presented separately – in a table, graph, bar chart or pie chart, for example. So that you can compare the different ways of presenting information, the same data are presented below in different formats.

Data presented in a table

FIGURE 1: **Number of earthquakes in the US (by magnitude)**

Magnitude	1998	1999	2000	2001
0.1–3.9	1,400	1,100	1,300	1,400
4.0–4.9	1,600	1,100	1,800	1,700
5.0–9.9	500	700	600	500
Total	3,500	2,900	3,700	3,600

Data presented in a bar chart

FIGURE 2: **Number of earthquakes in the US (by magnitude)**

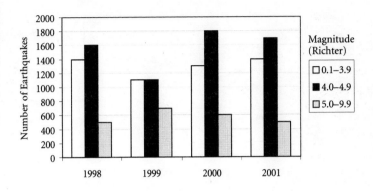

Below is another way of presenting the same data in a different type of bar chart.

FIGURE 3: **Number of earthquakes in the US (by magnitude)**

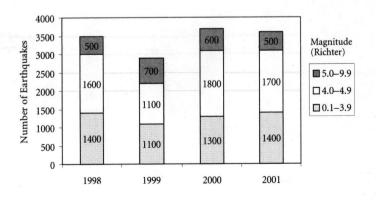

Data presented in a graph

FIGURE 4: Number of earthquakes in the US (by magnitude)

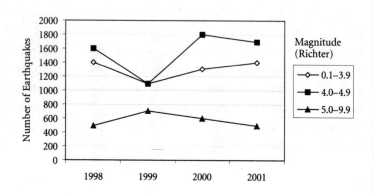

Data presented in pie charts

FIGURE 5: Number of earthquakes in the US in 1998 (by magnitude)

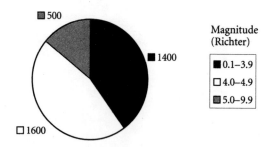

These are a few ways in which data can be presented, and they are, in fact, the most common ways in which data are presented in numerical reasoning tests. So what type of questions could you come across in a test that presents the numerical information in these formats?

Questions related to tables, graphs and so on could be simple questions that look at whether you are able to extract the relevant data from the table and perform simple calculations, but other questions will require you to extract data from the table and then perform calculations such as those presented in the Further Numerical Calculations section (see pages 38–87). In the following sections you will be presented with various practice questions that are linked to the different formats in which data can be presented.

Questions based on tables

Take as an example Figure 1, and solve the practice questions, rounding off your answers to the nearest whole number.

FIGURE 1 (repeated): **Number of earthquakes in the US (by magnitude)**

Magnitude	1998	1999	2000	2001
0.1–3.9	1,400	1,100	1,300	1,400
4.0–4.9	1,600	1,100	1,800	1,700
5.0–9.9	500	700	600	500
Total	3,500	2,900	3,700	3,600

Practice questions

QUESTION   ANSWER

185. How many more 0.1–3.9 earthquakes were there
     in 2000 than in 1999?

     a. 100
     b. 200
     c. 300
     d. 400
     e. 500

QUESTION   ANSWER

186. On average, how many 5.0–9.9 earthquakes were
there each year between 1998 and 2001?

    a. 500
    b. 525
    c. 550
    d. 575
    e. 600

QUESTION   ANSWER

187. By what percentage did the total number of
earthquakes decrease between 1998 and 1999?

    a. 14.9%
    b. 16.0%
    c. 17.1%
    d. 18.2%
    e. 19.3%

QUESTION   ANSWER

188. What percentage of the total earthquakes in 2001
were the 4.0–4.9 earthquakes?

    a. 45.0%
    b. 47.2%
    c. 49.4%
    d. 51.6%
    e. 53.8%

QUESTION   ANSWER

189. What was the ratio of 4.0–4.9 to 5.0–9.9
earthquakes in 2000?

   a. 3:1

   b. 3:2

   c. 3:4

   d. 2:3

   e. 1:3

QUESTION   ANSWER

190. What percentage of earthquakes in 2000 and 2001
combined were the 0.1–3.9 earthquakes?

   a. 31%

   b. 33%

   c. 35%

   d. 37%

   e. 39%

Pay attention to detail. The questions presented above were all straightforward. However, make sure that you do not make assumptions that
are not true. Look, for example, at the following questions.

QUESTION	ANSWER

191. How many more earthquakes were there in 2000 than in 1998?

    a. 100

    b. 200

    c. 300

    d. 600

    e. 800

Because you are in a hurry, you might assume that the question asks you about an increase between two consecutive years. This is not always the case.

QUESTION	ANSWER

192. On average, approximately how many 0.1–3.9 earthquakes were there a year between 1998 and 2000?

    a. 1,145

    b. 1,200

    c. 1,267

    d. 1,300

    e. 3,367

Again, you may assume that you are requested to calculate the average of all the values presented to you, but this is not always the case. So you have to make sure you pay attention to detail and look at the correct data.

FIGURE 6: **Ownership of cars (by household type)**

	1997		2001	
Type of household	No. of households (in thousands)	% of households owning a car	No. of households (in thousands)	% of households owning a car
1-person	870	42	960	68
2-person	690	75	710	82
3-person	330	92	310	94
4-person	300	95	290	97
5-person	70	96	70	97

Practice questions

....

QUESTION   ANSWER

193. How many four-person households owned a car in 1997?

    a. 281,300   **b.** 285,000   **c.** 288,500
    d. 291,400   **e.** 303,600

....

QUESTION   ANSWER

194. By approximately what percentage did the number of three-person households decrease from 1997 to 2001?

    a. 4%   **b.** 5%   **c.** 6%
    d. 8%   **e.** Cannot Say

....

QUESTION   ANSWER

195. How many people were living in a three- or a
four-person household in 2001?

    a. 930 thousand **b.** 980 thousand **c.** 1.16 million
    d. 2.25 million   **e.** 2.09 million

QUESTION   ANSWER

196. What was the approximate ratio of two to four-
person households in 2001?

    a. 2.40:1   **b.** 2.45:1   **c.** 2.66:1
    d. 2.75:1   **e.** Cannot Say

QUESTION   ANSWER

197. If the number of one-person households owning a
car increased by 10% each year from 2001, how
many were there in 2004?

    a. 718,080   **b.** 789,888   **c.** 829,382
    d. 868,877   **e.** Cannot Say

QUESTION	ANSWER

198. By approximately what percentage did the number of one-person households owning a car increase from 1997 to 2001?

    a. 10%   **b.** 26%   **c.** 58%

    d. 67%   **e.** 79%

'Cannot Say' option

The multiple-choice answers in numerical reasoning tests occasionally include a 'Cannot Say' option rather than a numerical response. You should choose this option if the information provided in the graph is not sufficient for you to calculate the answer. Try to solve the following question.

QUESTION	ANSWER

199. How many people, living in three-person households, owned a car in 1997?

    a. 303,600

    b. 530,000

    c. 910,800

    d. 990,000

    e. Cannot Say

The answer here is 'Cannot Say' because the table does not give you enough information to calculate this. Although it gives you the number of households owning a car and the number of people living in these households, you do not actually know how many of the people in each household own a car.

Questions for which the correct answer is 'Cannot Say' are often based on extrapolation. This means that from the information given, you could perform calculations in order to extrapolate the answer, but your answer would just be an estimation and not definitely the correct answer. Look, for example, at the question below, which is again linked to the data presented in Figure 6.

....

QUESTION	ANSWER
200. How many one-person households were there in 1999?	

    a. 900,000
    b. 914,000
    c. 915,000
    d. 920,000
    e. Cannot Say

....

The correct answer here is 'Cannot Say'. However, you could make estimations on how many households there could be. You could, for example, make an estimation based on the assumption that between 1997 and 2001 the increase in households was spread evenly over the years. So you could estimate that in 1997 there were 915,000 three-person households. However, there is no information in the data indicating that your assumption is correct. So, when there is a 'Cannot Say' option in the answers, make sure you do not make any assumptions in order to derive an answer. If you need to make an assumption to calculate an answer the correct answer is actually 'Cannot Say'.

Questions based on bar charts

FIGURE 7: **Imports and Exports for European Countries**

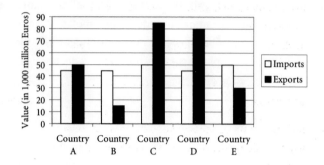

Practice questions

....

QUESTION   ANSWER

201. Which country has the greatest value of exports?

    a. Country A

    b. Country B

    c. Country C

    d. Country D

    e. Country E

....

QUESTION   ANSWER

202. What is the percentage of Country E's exports to
imports?

    a. 56%

    b. 60%

    c. 76%

    d. 106%

    e. 166%

....

QUESTION   ANSWER

203. By what percentage would Country A's imports
need to increase in order to equal the value of its
exports?

a. 8.5%   **b.** 9.0%   **c.** 10.0%

d. 11.1%   **e.** 12.2%

QUESTION   ANSWER

204. If Country B's imports were to decrease by 10%
what would be the difference between its imports
and exports?

a. 23,500 million euros   **b.** 25,500 million euros

c. 26,000 million euros   **d.** 28,500 million euros

e. 34,500 million euros

QUESTION   ANSWER

205. If 15% of Country D's imports are from Country
A, what value of goods does Country A export to
other countries, apart from Country D?

a. €35,750 million   **b.** €38,250 million

c. €39,500 million   **d.** €40,250 million

e. €43,250 million

QUESTION   ANSWER

206. What percentage of the total exports made by
these five countries was made by Country C?

a. 31%   **b.** 33%   **c.** 35%

d. 37%   **e.** 39%

FIGURE 8: Sales of electrical goods in 2006

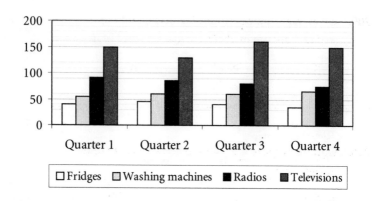

Practice questions

QUESTION   ANSWER

207. On average how many televisions were sold each
month during the first quarter of 2006?

    a. 47   **b.** 48   **c.** 49

    d. 50   **e.** 51

QUESTION   ANSWER

208. In which quarter of the year was the greatest
number of electrical goods sold?

    a. Quarter 1   **b.** Quarter 2   **c.** Quarter 3

    d. Quarter 4   **e.** Cannot Say

QUESTION   ANSWER

209. On average how many washing machines were
sold each month of 2006?

 a. 20   **b.** 24   **c.** 28

 d. 32   **e.** 36

QUESTION   ANSWER

210. How many more televisions than radios were sold
during 2006?

 a. 220   **b.** 240   **c.** 260

 d. 280   **e.** 300

QUESTION   ANSWER

211. In the first half of 2006 proportionately how many
more washing machines than fridges were sold?

 a. 23%   **b.** 27%   **c.** 31%

 d. 35%   **e.** 39%

QUESTION   ANSWER

212. The shop sold £60,000 worth of fridges during the
year, what was the average price of a fridge?

 a. £365   **b.** £375   **c.** £385

 d. £395   **e.** £405

Questions based on graphs

FIGURE 9: Room Occupancy for Hotel Grand (20 rooms)

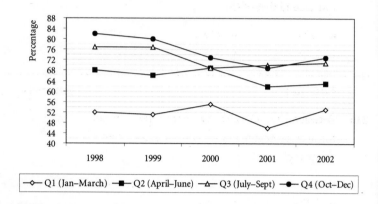

─◇─ Q1 (Jan–March)   ─■─ Q2 (April–June)   ─△─ Q3 (July–Sept)   ─●─ Q4 (Oct–Dec)

Practice questions

....

QUESTION   ANSWER

213. What was the average Q1 occupancy rate between
1998 and 2002?

    a. 50.6%   **b.** 50.8%   **c.** 51.0%

    d. 51.2%   **e.** 51.4%

....

QUESTION   ANSWER

214. What was the occupancy rate of the Grand Hotel
in January 2000?

    a. 50%   **b.** 52%   **c.** 55%

    d. 57%   **e.** Cannot Say

....

QUESTION   ANSWER

215. In 1999 by what proportion did the Q3 occupancy
rate exceed that of Q1?

    a. 37%   **b.** 42%   **c.** 47%

    d. 51%   **e.** 56%

QUESTION   ANSWER

216. Between 1999 and 2001 by what proportion did
the average occupancy rate for the second half of
the year change?

    a. −11.5%   **b.** −9.7%   **c.** −8.3%

    d. 5.4%   **e.** 9.2%

QUESTION   ANSWER

217. On average by how much did the Q4 occupancy
rate reduce each year between 1998 and 2002?

    a. 1.65%   **b.** 1.80%   **c.** 2.05%

    d. 2.25%   **e.** 2.40%

QUESTION   ANSWER

218. If room rates increased by 5% between 2000 and
2001, by what proportion would the Q1 income
change between these years?

    a. −10.8%   **b.** −11.5%   **c.** −12.2%

    d. −13.2%   **e.** −16.4%

FIGURE 10: **Revenue by company**

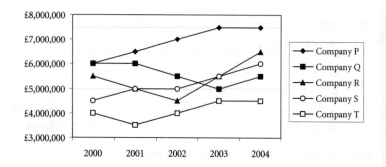

Practice questions

QUESTION   ANSWER

219. What was the average revenue earned by the five
companies in 2001?

    a. £5.0 million
    b. £5.2 million
    c. £5.4 million
    d. £5.6 million
    e. £5.8 million

QUESTION   ANSWER

220. In 2000 Company P had 12% of the total market.
What was the total market worth?

    a. 50 million
    b. 51 million
    c. 52 million
    d. 53 million
    e. 54 million

QUESTION ANSWER

221. Which company had the second highest average revenue across all five years?

a. Company P **b.** Company Q **c.** Company R
d. Company S **e.** Company T

QUESTION ANSWER

222. Between 2001 and 2004 which company proportionately increased its revenue the most?

a. Company P **b.** Company Q **c.** Company R
d. Company S **e.** Company T

QUESTION ANSWER

223. If the percentage increase in Company Q's revenue between 2003 and 2004 is the same in the following year, what will Company Q's revenue be in 2005?

a. £6.00 million **b.** £6.05 million **c.** £6.10 million
d. £6.15 million **e.** £6.20 million

QUESTION ANSWER

224. If the percentage increase in the revenue of Company P and Company S from 2003 to 2004 continues for the next five years, in which year will the revenue of Company S exceed that of Company P?

a. 2005 **b.** 2006 **c.** 2007
d. 2008 **e.** 2009

Questions based on pie charts

FIGURE 11: **Company costs by department**

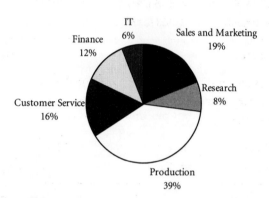

Annual Expenditure
£2,500,000

Practice questions

....

QUESTION   ANSWER

225. What proportion of the annual expenditure is
accounted for by functions other than Production
and Customer Services?

    a. 42%   **b.** 45%   **c.** 48%
    d. 51%   **e.** 55%

....

QUESTION   ANSWER

226. On average approximately how much is spent each
month on the Research Department?

    a. £1,725   **b.** £2,500   **c.** £16,667
    d. £31,000   **e.** £200,000

....

QUESTION	ANSWER

227. Next year the Sales and Marketing budget will increase by 4%. What will the new budget be for Sales and Marketing?

    a. £474,000   **b.** £484,000   **c.** £494,000
    d. £504,000   **e.** £514,000

QUESTION	ANSWER

228. Next year a further £40,000 will be invested in IT. If the overall budget increases by 2%, what proportion will be accounted for by IT?

    a. 6.1%   **b.** 6.9%   **c.** 7.1%
    d. 7.5%   **e.** 7.7%

QUESTION	ANSWER

229. If the Production budget increases by 2% and Customer Service decreases by 3%, by what percentage will the overall expenditure change if those of other departments are unchanged?

    a. −0.40%   **b.** −0.20%   **c.** 0.10%
    d. 0.20%   **e.** 0.30%

QUESTION	ANSWER

230. If the annual expenditure increases by 5% in two years and the total expenditure on research and IT becomes £550,000, what percentage of the overall expenditure will be due to research?

    a. 6%   **b.** 7%   **c.** 8%
    d. 10%   **e.** Cannot Say

FIGURE 12: **Population composition for North and South Regions**

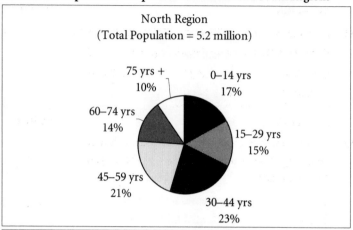

North Region
(Total Population = 5.2 million)

75 yrs +
10%

0–14 yrs
17%

60–74 yrs
14%

15–29 yrs
15%

45–59 yrs
21%

30–44 yrs
23%

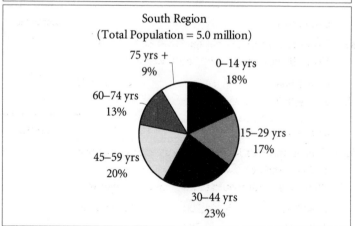

South Region
(Total Population = 5.0 million)

75 yrs +
9%

0–14 yrs
18%

60–74 yrs
13%

15–29 yrs
17%

45–59 yrs
20%

30–44 yrs
23%

Practice questions

QUESTION   ANSWER

231. How many 60–74-year-olds live in the South
Region?

    a. 500,000   **b.** 550,000   **c.** 600,000

    d. 650,000   **e.** 700,000

QUESTION   ANSWER

232. How many more 15–29-year-olds live in the South
Region compared to the North Region?

    a. 70,000   **b.** 72,000   **c.** 74,000
    d. 76,000   **e.** 78,000

QUESTION   ANSWER

233. For the North Region, what is the proportion of
people aged 60 or older compared to those aged
29 or younger?

    a. 4:1   **b.** 4:3   **c.** 3:4
    d. 2:4   **e.** 1:4

QUESTION   ANSWER

234. How many more people aged over 60 live in the
North Region than in the South Region?

    a. 140,000   **b.** 142,000   **c.** 144,000
    d. 146,000   **e.** 148,000

QUESTION   ANSWER

235. If the number of 30–59-year-olds were to increase
by 2% in the next five years, how many more
30–59-year-olds would there be in both regions?

    a. 88,700   **b.** 88,720   **c.** 88,740
    d. 88,760   **e.** 88,780

QUESTION   ANSWER

236. If the number of people under 30 were to decrease
by 1% in the next ten years, how many people
under 30 would there be in both regions?

    a. 34,140   **b.** 68,280   **c.** 1,842,690
    d. 2,573,160   **e.** 3,379,860

Other numerical questions

Number sequences

A different type of question that you may find in a numerical test is one that is based on number sequences. A sequence is a string of values that follows some pattern, and these questions will typically give you several numbers in a row and ask you to find either the missing number or the next number in the sequence.

The more you practise solving questions on sequences, the easier they will become. This is because sequences often follow specific patterns, and if you have already found a pattern once, it will be easier to observe it again with different numbers.

Practice questions
Find the number that should replace '?' in the following sequences.

....

QUESTION	ANSWER

237.   64, 49, 36, ?, 16, 9 . . .

   a. 21
   b. 23
   c. 25
   d. 27
   e. 29

....

QUESTION	ANSWER

238.   1, 3, ?, 10, 15, 21 . . .

   a. 5
   b. 6
   c. 7
   d. 8
   e. 8

....

| QUESTION | ANSWER |

239. 3, 9, 27, 81, ?, 729 . . .

    a. 108
    b. 141
    c. 167
    d. 243
    e. 324

| QUESTION | ANSWER |

240. 5, 6, 4, 7, 3, 8, ? . . .

    a. 1
    b. 2
    c. 5
    d. 9
    e. 13

| QUESTION | ANSWER |

241. 1, 4, ?, 22, 46, 94, 190 . . .

    a. 10
    b. 11
    c. 12
    d. 13
    e. 14

QUESTION   ANSWER

242. 1, 5, 9, 13, 17, ?, 25, 29, 33 . . .

    a. 19
    b. 20
    c. 21
    d. 22
    e. 23

QUESTION   ANSWER

243. 1, 3, 7, 13, 21, 31, ? . . .

    a. 39
    b. 40
    c. 41
    d. 42
    e. 43

QUESTION   ANSWER

244. 60, 58, ?, 48, 40, 30 . . .

    a. 52
    b. 53
    c. 54
    d. 55
    e. 56

| QUESTION | ANSWER |

245. 2, 3, 5, 8, 12, 17, 23, ?, 38 . . .

    a. 27
    b. 28
    c. 29
    d. 30
    e. 31

| QUESTION | ANSWER |

246. 41, 38, 35, 32, ?, 26, 23 . . .

    a. 27
    b. 28
    c. 29
    d. 30
    e. 31

| QUESTION | ANSWER |

247. 2, 4, 8, 14, 22, 32, 44, 58, ? . . .

    a. 68
    b. 72
    c. 74
    d. 76
    e. 78

QUESTION   **ANSWER**

248.   2, 3, 6, 7, 14, 15, 30, 31, 62, 63, ? . . .

    a. 64

    b. 66

    c. 94

    d. 112

    e. 126

QUESTION   **ANSWER**

249.   2, 1, ?, 2, 4, 3, 5, 4, 6, 5 . . .

    a. 1

    b. 2

    c. 3

    d. 4

    e. 5

QUESTION   **ANSWER**

250.   9, 16, 23, 30, ?, 44, 51, 58 . . .

    a. 33

    b. 34

    c. 35

    d. 36

    e. 37

QUESTION   ANSWER

251. 7, 15, 18, 25, 29, 35, 40, 45, ?, 55, 62 . . .

    a. 48

    b. 49

    c. 50

    d. 51

    e. 52

QUESTION   ANSWER

252. 12, 9, 11, 7, 10, 5, 9, 3, 8, ? . . .

    a. 1

    b. 2

    c. 3

    d. 5

    e. 7

QUESTION   ANSWER

253. 4, 5, 8, 13, 20, ?, 40, 53 . . .

    a. 25

    b. 27

    c. 29

    d. 31

    e. 33

QUESTION   ANSWER

254.   9.1, 10.8, 12.5, 14.2, 15.9, ?, 19.3 . . .

    a. 17.0

    b. 17.2

    c. 17.4

    d. 17.6

    e. 17.8

QUESTION   ANSWER

255.   1, 4, 5, 9, 14, 23, ?, 60, 97, 157 . . .

    a. 37

    b. 43

    c. 47

    d. 52

    e. 56

QUESTION   ANSWER

256.   1, −1, −2, 6, 24, ?, −720 . . .

    a. −120

    b. −64

    c. 64

    d. 120

    e. 540

| QUESTION | ANSWER |

257. 1, 2, 4, 7, 11, 16, 22, ?, 37 . . .

    a. 27
    b. 28
    c. 29
    d. 30
    e. 31

| QUESTION | ANSWER |

258. 23, 19, 17, ?, 11, 7, 5, 1 . . .

    a. 12
    b. 13
    c. 14
    d. 15
    e. 16

| QUESTION | ANSWER |

259. 11, 101, 25, 242, 39, 383, 53, 524, 67, ? . . .

    a. 81
    b. 573
    c. 607
    d. 627
    e. 665

QUESTION   ANSWER

260. 2, 5, 1, 4, 0, ?, −1, 2, −2, 1, −3 . . .

   a. −1
   b. 1
   c. 2
   d. 3
   e. 4

Other non-graphical questions

Graphical questions are very common in numerical tests, but other types of questions can also be asked. Sometimes they involve a combination of different calculations. It's difficult to think of a way of grouping these sorts of questions together, as every test-setter has a different way of combining calculations. The important thing to remember is that you have already practised all the skills you need to answer these questions, so you just have to pay attention and combine the skills in the correct way. The following section will give you a chance to practise some questions involving non-graphical information.

Practice questions

QUESTION   ANSWER

261. If one proof-reader can proof-read two pages in three minutes, how many minutes would it take four proof-readers to proof-read 12 pages?

   a. 0.75 minutes
   b. 3 minutes
   c. 4.5 minutes
   d. 12 minutes
   e. 18 minutes

QUESTION	ANSWER

262. A car's speed averages at 30 mph for one hour, after which the car's speed is constant at 70 mph for the next two hours. How far has the car travelled?

    a. 100 miles
    b. 130 miles
    c. 140 miles
    d. 160 miles
    e. 170 miles

QUESTION	ANSWER

263. In 70 minutes' time it will be half as close to noon as it is now. What time is it now?

    a. 9:40
    b. 10:00
    c. 10:25
    d. 10:50
    e. 11:30

QUESTION	ANSWER

264. An electrical store buys 40 televisions at £63.29 each and twice as many radios at £25.99 each. How much remains from a budget of £5,000?

    a. £299.00
    b. £389.20
    c. £526.40
    d. £1,087.60
    e. £4,610.80

QUESTION   **ANSWER**

265. A company has profits of £60,000, of which 20%
will be paid as tax. The remaining profit will be
split between four owners, of whom one owns as
much as the other three together. How much will
the majority owner receive?

   a. £8,000
   b. £12,000
   c. £16,000
   d. £24,000
   e. £48,000

QUESTION   **ANSWER**

266. If a company makes 700 mugs in a five-day
working week, when a day has 7 working hours,
how many mugs are made in one hour?

   a. 10
   b. 20
   c. 30
   d. 40
   e. 50

QUESTION   **ANSWER**

267. A page of stickers measures 24 cm by 30 cm. If each
sticker is 4 cm by 6 cm, what is the maximum number
of stickers that will fit on the page with no overlap?

   a. 22
   b. 24
   c. 26
   d. 28
   e. 30

QUESTION	ANSWER

268. Fountain pens cost twice as much as gel pens, which are one and a half times the cost of ballpoint pens. If a ballpoint pen costs £1.50, how many fountain pens can you get for £14.00?

   a. 2

   b. 3

   c. 4

   d. 5

   e. 6

QUESTION	ANSWER

269. Four women go for drinks and they each order a coffee for £2.69 and a muffin for 85p. If one woman paid with a £20 note for all the food and drinks, how much change would she get?

   a. £3.54

   b. £5.84

   c. £9.24

   d. £10.76

   e. £14.16

QUESTION   ANSWER

270. In a factory that manufactures toasters, 20% of
all those made are black and 40% are silver. If
800 toasters are made per week, how many black
and silver toasters will have been made in one
year?

    a. 24,900

    b. 24,920

    c. 24,940

    d. 24,960

    e. 24,980

QUESTION   ANSWER

271. A coach took 30 minutes to finish a journey. If it
travelled at an average speed of 50 mph, how far
did it travel?

    a. 20 miles

    b. 25 miles

    c. 30 miles

    d. 35 miles

    e. 40 miles

QUESTION   ANSWER

272. How many bananas can you buy with £2.10 if a
banana costs 32p?

    a. 4

    b. 5

    c. 6

    d. 7

    e. 8

QUESTION	ANSWER

273. A photocopier copies 30 pages a minute. How long will it take to make 25 copies of a document 90 pages long?

    a. 1 hour
    b. 1.25 hours
    c. 1.50 hours
    d. 1.75 hours
    e. 2 hours

QUESTION	ANSWER

274. How many 25 cl cups of water can be filled from a 200 cl bottle?

    a. 5
    b. 6
    c. 7
    d. 8
    e. 9

QUESTION	ANSWER

275. For every three packets of crisps bought, you receive one packet extra free. If each packet costs 40p each, how much would you pay for 20 packets?

    a. £6
    b. £7
    c. £8
    d. £9
    e. £10

QUESTION   ANSWER

276. A clock gains 2 minutes every hour. If it is
currently four hours ahead, for how long has it
been gaining time?

  a. 20 hours
  b. 2 days
  c. 3 days 10 hours
  d. 5 days
  e. 8 days 8 hours

QUESTION   ANSWER

277. How many 20 cm by 20 cm tiles would it take to
cover a wall 2 m by 2 m?

  a. 10
  b. 20
  c. 80
  d. 100
  e. 200

QUESTION   ANSWER

278. A file contains a 12,000-word document. If it took
the author 4 hours to write each page and each
page contained 750 words, how long did it take to
write the whole document?

  a. 16 hours
  b. 32 hours
  c. 64 hours
  d. 68 hours
  e. 72 hours

QUESTION   ANSWER

279. If you paid £528.75, including 17.5% VAT, for a
computer, how much did the computer cost
before VAT was added?

   a. £354
   b. £450
   c. £462
   d. £465
   e. £470

QUESTION   ANSWER

280. Five diners each had a starter, a main course and a
drink, resulting in a total bill of £200. If the
starters were an average of £7 each and the main
courses an average of £22, how much on average
was spent on drinks?

   a. £11
   b. £12
   c. £13
   d. £14
   e. £15

4 Practice tests

You have now gone through the majority of the different types of question that you can come across in a numerical reasoning test. You have seen the solutions for most of them worked out step by step and you have practised the calculations required for each type and solved various example questions.

In the following pages you will find five numerical tests, each consisting of 24 questions and in a format that is commonly used by companies in their recruitment process. These will help you practise numerical tests in a more formal way. The number of questions in numerical tests is not fixed, but 24 items is fairly standard. The tests here include a mixture of different ways of presenting data and also a variety of types of question.

We would suggest that you take each test with a time limit of 24 minutes. When the time is up, mark the question you have reached and continue with the remaining questions. This will give you an idea of what it will be like under test conditions. Do not feel overwhelmed if you do not finish the questions within the allotted time. The time allowed for numerical tests is such that it is difficult for a person to solve all the questions in time.

If you do not feel 'ready' to complete the tests under proper test conditions just yet, you can make the switch from practising with questions to practising with actual tests a bit more gradual. You could, for example, take the first two tests without setting the 24-minute limit, which will allow you to familiarize yourself with putting together everything that you have learned in the previous chapter. You should still, however, solve the questions as quickly as possible if you want to make the most of these tests. Once you have done this, you should then have a go with the remaining three tests, setting the 24-minute time limit for yourself.

Practice test 1

FIGURE 13: Cotton industry in 2003

	Export ('000 bales)	Import ('000 bales)	Production ('000 bales)	Per capita production*	Use ('000 bales)
Argentina	50	100	475	1.2	525
Brazil	1,300	300	4,400	2.36	3,650
China	150	4,300	25,500	1.95	30,400
India	50	1,250	12,500	1.16	13,500
Peru	10	200	184	0.66	380

* = 1,000 bales per 100,000 people

....

QUESTION   ANSWER

281. In 2003 what percentage of the cotton used in
Brazil was imported?

a. 4.9%   **b.** 6.0%   **c.** 7.1%

d. 8.2%   **e.** 9.3%

....

QUESTION   ANSWER

282. Approximately what was the population of
Argentina in 2003?

a. 39.2 million   **b.** 39.4 million   **c.** 39.6 million

d. 39.8 million   **e.** 40 million

....

QUESTION   ANSWER

283. Which country exported the second highest proportion of its production of cotton in 2003?

a. Argentina   **b.** Brazil   **c.** China
d. India   **e.** Peru

QUESTION   ANSWER

284. In 2003 what was the use of cotton per capita in India (1,000 bales per 100,000 people)?

a. 1.05   **b.** 1.15   **c.** 1.25
d. 1.35   **e.** 1.45

QUESTION   ANSWER

285. If the area of China is 9.6 million square kilometres, what was its population density in 2003?

a. 135.1 people/km^2 **b.** 136.2 people/km^2
c. 137.3 people/km^2 **d.** 138.4 people/km^2
e. 139.5 people/km^2

QUESTION   ANSWER

286. Peru produced 30% more cotton in 2004 than in 2003 and exported 5% of this. If usage remained constant, how much cotton did Peru import in 2004 (in 1,000 bales)?

a. 144 320 bales   **b.** 146 430 bales
c. 148 540 bales   **d.** 150 650 bales
e. 152 760 bales

FIGURE 14: **Destination of first degree graduates in the UK**

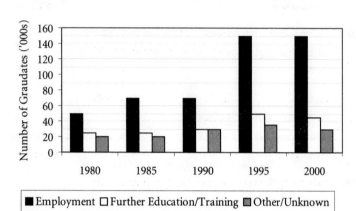

....

QUESTION   ANSWER

287. In which year did the highest number of graduates
go on to destinations other than employment?

  a. 1980
  b. 1985
  c. 1990
  d. 1995
  e. 2000

....

QUESTION   ANSWER

288. How many graduates were there in 1995?

  a. 231,000
  b. 233,000
  c. 235,000
  d. 237,000
  e. 239,000

....

| QUESTION | ANSWER |

289. What was the percentage increase in the number of graduates going into employment from 1990 to 1995?

   a. 14%   **b.** 47%   **c.** 66%
   d. 114%   **e.** 214%

| QUESTION | ANSWER |

290. What was the ratio of the number of graduates going on to further education/training to other/unknown destinations in 2000?

   a. 3:1   **b.** 3:2   **c.** 5:3
   d. 2:3   **e.** 1:3

| QUESTION | ANSWER |

291. If the total number of graduates decreased by the same number each year from 1995 to 2000, how many graduates were there in 1998?

   a. 221,000   **b.** 223,000   **c.** 225,000
   d. 227,000   **e.** 229,000

| QUESTION | ANSWER |

292. What proportion of graduates in 1990 went on to further education/training?

   a. 23.08%   **b.** 25.37%   **c.** 27.84%
   d. 30.00%   **e.** 32.16%

FIGURE 15: Capacities for nuclear electricity generation

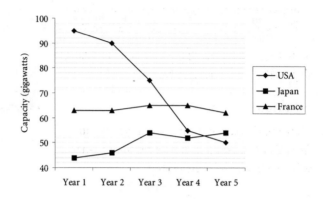

....

QUESTION   ANSWER

293. In which year was there the greatest difference in
the capacity for nuclear generation between the
USA and France and Japan combined?

a. Year 1   **b.** Year 2   **c.** Year 3
d. Year 4   **e.** Year 5

....

QUESTION   ANSWER

294. Over the five years, on average, what was the
capacity for nuclear generation per year in the
USA (in gigawatts)?

a. 71   **b.** 73   **c.** 75
d. 77   **e.** 79

....

QUESTION	ANSWER

295. What was the percentage increase in capacity for nuclear generation for Japan from Year 2 to Year 4?

   a. 10.01%   **b.** 11.02%   **c.** 12.03%

   d. 13.04%   **e.** 14.05%

QUESTION	ANSWER

296. If the trend in capacity for nuclear generation from Year 4 to Year 5 in France continues, what will it be in Year 8 (in gigawatts)?

   a. 51   **b.** 52   **c.** 53

   d. 54   **e.** 55

QUESTION	ANSWER

297. The ratio of the capacity for nuclear electricity generation from the USA to Japan in Year 3 is the same in Year 6, and the capacity in the USA in Year 6 is 30% greater than that in Year 5. What is the capacity for nuclear generation in Japan in Year 6 (in gigawatts)?

   a. 40.2   **b.** 42.4   **c.** 44.6

   d. 46.8   **e.** 49

QUESTION	ANSWER

298. If these three countries together made up 57% of the total world capacity for nuclear generation in Year 1, what was the total world capacity in Year 1 (in gigawatts)?

   a. 354.4   **b.** 355.5   **c.** 356.6

   d. 357.7   **e.** 358.8

FIGURE 16: **Total temporary employment**

2000
Total Temporary Employment: 1,653,044

Other
12%

Seasonal
4%

Agency temping
16%

Fixed-period
contract
48%

Casual work
20%

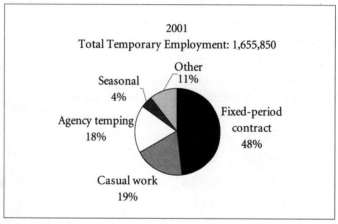

2001
Total Temporary Employment: 1,655,850

Other
11%

Seasonal
4%

Agency temping
18%

Fixed-period
contract
48%

Casual work
19%

QUESTION   ANSWER

299. Approximately how many temporary workers
were on fixed-period contracts in 2001?

a. 794,800   b. 794,810   c. 794,820

d. 794,830   e. 794,840

QUESTION   ANSWER

300. What was the ratio of agency temporary workers
to casual workers in 2000?

    a. 3:5   **b.** 4:5   **c.** 16:20

    d. 5:4   **e.** 20:16

QUESTION   ANSWER

301. What was the total number of casual workers in
both years combined?

    a. 645,220   **b.** 645,240   **c.** 645,260

    d. 645,280   **e.** 645,300

QUESTION   ANSWER

302. What was the percentage increase in the number
of agency temporary workers from 2000 to 2001?

    a. 2%   **b.** 5%   **c.** 8%

    d. 10%   **e.** 13%

QUESTION   ANSWER

303. In 2000 approximately how many temporary
workers were on fixed-period contracts or in other
temporary employment?

    a. 991,810   **b.** 991,820   **c.** 991,830

    d. 991,840   **e.** 991,850

QUESTION   ANSWER

304. If 58% of the seasonal workers worked over the
summer period in 2000 and 62% worked over the
summer period in 2001, in total, approximately
how many seasonal workers were there in the two
summers combined?

    a. 79,400   **b.** 79,410   **c.** 79,420

    d. 79,430   **e.** 79,440

Practice test 2

FIGURE 17: Population distributed by age

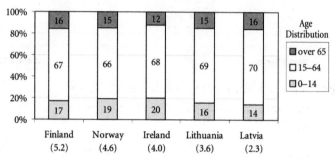

| QUESTION | ANSWER |

305. How many people in Norway are aged above 65?

    a. 680,000   **b.** 690,000   **c.** 700,000

    d. 710,000   **e.** 720,000

| QUESTION | ANSWER |

306. What is the population on average for the five countries presented?

    a. 3.9 million   **b.** 4.0 million   **c.** 4.1 million

    d. 4.2 million   **e.** 4.3 million

QUESTION   ANSWER

307. How many Irish people are over 14?

    a. 3,100,000   **b.** 3,120,000   **c.** 3,160,000
    d. 3,185,000   **e.** 3,200,000

QUESTION   ANSWER

308. If the population of Finland increases by 0.14%
each year, how much will it be in 4 years from
now?

    a. 5,214,570   **b.** 5,221,871   **c.** 5,229,120
    d. 5,229,181   **e.** 5,232,213

QUESTION   ANSWER

309. What is the ratio of people aged 15 to 64 in
Ireland to those in Lithuania?

    a. 1.1:1   **b.** 1.2:1   **c.** 1.3:1
    d. 1.4:1   **e.** 1.5:1

QUESTION   ANSWER

310. If the population of Latvia decreases by 0.67% next
year and the ratio of the population aged below 15
to the rest of the population remains constant, how
many people will be aged below 15 next year?

    a. 227,650   **b.** 319,843   **c.** 340,455
    d. 342,689   **e.** 345,000

FIGURE 18: Air pollution by country

	Sulphur oxides		Nitrogen oxides		Population	
	kg per capita (in 1990)	Change in kg per capita 1990/2002 (%)	kg per capita (in 1990)	Change in kg per capita 1990/2002 (%)	in 1990 (millions)	in 2002 (millions)
Czech Republic	165	−85	50	−40	10	10.1
Finland	100	−65	60	−30	5	5.1
France	65	−60	35	−30	59.5	60.5
Germany	35	−90	30	−50	81	82.2
United Kingdom	135	−75	40	−40	59	60.2

....

QUESTION   ANSWER

311. What was the ratio of the population of the UK to the population of Germany in 2002?

    a. 1.24:1   **b.** 1.29:1   **c.** 1.37:1

    d. 1.39:1   **e.** 1.42:1

....

QUESTION   ANSWER

312. How much was the per capita production of sulphur oxides in Finland in 2002?

    a. 3.5 kg   **b.** 24.75 kg   **c.** 26 kg

    d. 33.75 kg   **e.** 35 kg

....

QUESTION   ANSWER

313. On average how much was the per capita
production of nitrogen oxides of the five countries
in 1990?

a. 41 kg   **b.** 42 kg   **c.** 43 kg
d. 44 kg   **e.** 45 kg

QUESTION   ANSWER

314. How many kilograms of nitrogen oxides were
produced by the Czech Republic and by Finland in
2002?

a. 510,500,000 kg   **b.** 512,000,000 kg
c. 515,400,000 kg   **d.** 517,200,000 kg
e. 520,600,000 kg

QUESTION   ANSWER

315. What was the ratio of sulphur oxides to nitrogen
oxides produced in the United Kingdom in 2002?

a. 0.71:1   **b.** 1.12:1   **c.** 1.25:1
d. 1.41:1   **e.** 1.92:1

QUESTION   ANSWER

316. If the total production of sulphur oxides in the
Czech Republic decreased by 10% from 2002 to
2004 and the population increased by 0.05%, how
much was the per capita production of sulphur
oxides in 2004?

a. 22.26 kg   **b.** 22.46 kg   **c.** 22.75 kg
d. 22.85 kg   **e.** 22.94 kg

FIGURE 19: **Age at marriage**

	1989		1999	
	Men	Women	Men	Women
under 25	85,000	110,000	60,000	85,000
25–34	50,000	30,000	65,000	46,000
35–44	10,000	7,500	15,000	12,000
45 and over	5,000	2,500	6,000	3,000

QUESTION   ANSWER

317. From 1989 to 1999 what was the percentage decrease in the number of men who got married under the age of 35?

    a. 7.4%

    b. 7.6%

    c. 7.8%

    d. 8.0%

    e. 8.2%

QUESTION   ANSWER

318. How many more women got married in 1989 than in 1999?

    a. 4,000

    b. 5,000

    c. 6,000

    d. 8,000

    e. 10,000

QUESTION   ANSWER

319. What was the ratio of men to women who got
married aged under 25 in 1999?

    a. 0.5:1   **b.** 0.7:1   **c.** 0.8:1

    d. 1.1:1   **e.** 1.4:1

QUESTION   ANSWER

320. What percentage of the men who got married in
1999 were aged over 35?

    a. 8%   **b.** 10%   **c.** 12%

    d. 14%   **e.** 16%

QUESTION   ANSWER

321. By what percentage did the average age of getting
married increase for women from 1989 to 1999?

    a. 2.33%   **b.** 2.67%   **c.** 3.09%

    d. 3.12%   **e.** Cannot Say

QUESTION   ANSWER

322. If the number of marriages decreased from 1999
to 2005 by the same percentage as they decreased
from 1989 to 1999, how many marriages were
there in 2005?

    a. 141,259   **b.** 141,730   **c.** 141,955

    d. 142,107   **e.** 143,355

FIGURE 20: Labour force

	Population	Labour force	% of labour force by occupation		
			Industry	Service	Other
Finland	5,200,000	2,600,000	5	42	53
Hungary	9,800,000	4,200,000	32	65	3
Sweden	9,000,000	4,600,000	24	74	2
Austria	8,000,000	3,500,000	30	67	3

QUESTION   ANSWER

323. What percentage of the population in Finland is in the labour force?

    a. 43%

    b. 44%

    c. 48%

    d. 50%

    e. 51%

QUESTION   ANSWER

324. Approximately what percentage of the total population of Austria is working in the industry sector?

    a. 0.05%

    b. 12.2%

    c. 13.1%

    d. 13.7%

    e. 30.0%

QUESTION   ANSWER

325. In Hungary what is the ratio of people working in the services to the people working in the industry sector?

    a. 0.49:1   **b.** 1.82:1   **c.** 1.91:1
    d. 1.97:1   **e.** 2.03:1

QUESTION   ANSWER

326. If the ratio of men to women working in services in Sweden is 1.3:1, how many women are there working in services?

    a. 1,240,000   **b.** 1,480,000   **c.** 1,924,000
    d. 3,404,000   **e.** 3,913,043

QUESTION   ANSWER

327. If the labour force in Hungary increases by 1% each year but the percentages of the labour force remain constant within each sector, approximately how many people will be in the services sector in 2 years?

    a. 2,784,873   **b.** 2,791,357   **c.** 2,802,446
    d. 2,805,751   **e.** 2,809,292

QUESTION   ANSWER

328. If in Finland 15% of the other occupations are in the agriculture sector, what percentage of the total labour force is the agricultural sector?

    a. 3%   **b.** 4%   **c.** 6%
    d. 8%   **e.** 9%

Practice test 3

FIGURE 21: Price per ticket

	Full price	Concessions (Students/ unemployed people)
Front Row	£45.00	£22.50
Stalls	£35.00	£17.50
Circle	£25.00	£12.50
Upper Circle	£35.00	£15.00
Balcony	£25.00	£10.00

Practice questions

QUESTION   ANSWER

329. How much would three full-price and four
concessions tickets for the front row cost?

    a. £180.00   **b.** £202.50   **c.** £225.00
    d. £236.25   **e.** £247.50

QUESTION   ANSWER

330. How many concessions tickets for the upper circle
could be bought for £205?

    a. 13   **b.** 14   **c.** 15
    d. 16   **e.** 17

QUESTION   ANSWER

331. How much would 12 full-price tickets for the stalls
cost if the purchaser received a discount of 7.5%?

    a. £365.50   **b.** £388.50   **c.** £420.00
    d. £455.00   **e.** £499.50

QUESTION   ANSWER

332. A purchaser has been charged for eight full-price
tickets for the stalls instead of eight full-price
tickets for the balcony. How much have they paid
compared to what they should have paid?

    a. £80 less   **b.** £40 less   **c.** The same
    d. £40 more   **e.** £80 more

QUESTION   ANSWER

333. For which type of seat are concessions tickets sold
at the greatest percentage reduction?

    a. Front row   **b.** Stalls   **c.** Circle
    d. Upper circle   **e.** Balcony

QUESTION   ANSWER

334. A purchaser spends £100 for three full-price
tickets and two concessions tickets. Which type of
seat has he purchased tickets for?

    a. Front row   **b.** Stalls   **c.** Circle
    d. Upper circle   **e.** Balcony

FIGURE 22: Costs for the toll road

	One way	Monthly commuter ticket
Cars	$4.00	$80.00
Motorcycles	$2.00	$44.00
Caravans	$8.00	$168.00
Coaches	$20.00	$400.00
Lorries	$22.50	$427.50

Practice questions

QUESTION   ANSWER

335. How many one-way tickets could a car driver buy
     for the price of an equivalent coach ticket?

     a. 2   **b.** 3   **c.** 4
     d. 5   **e.** 6

QUESTION   ANSWER

336. The price for a one-way ticket for a lorry increases
     by 3.75%. How much does it cost after the increase?

     a. $23.34   **b.** $24.28   **c.** $25.59
     d. $26.25   **e.** $27.43

QUESTION   ANSWER

337. One toll booth is devoted entirely to cars buying
one-way tickets. If it can handle six cars per
minute on average, how much revenue could it
generate in 3 hours?

  a. $1440   **b.** $2160   **c.** $3450
  d. $4320   **e.** None of these

QUESTION   ANSWER

338. Four vehicles bought one-way tickets and paid a
total of $38. What were the four vehicles?

  a. 1 lorry, 3 cars   **b.** 1 coach, 2 caravans, 1 car
  c. 1 coach, 1 caravan, 1 car, 1 motorcycle
  d. 1 lorry, 2 cars, 1 caravan
  e. 1 coach, 2 caravans, 1 motorcycle

QUESTION   ANSWER

339. Which monthly ticket offers the greatest
percentage discount over the one-way tickets?

  a. Cars   **b.** Motorcycles   **c.** Caravans
  d. Coaches   **e.** Lorries

QUESTION   ANSWER

340. A commuter purchases a monthly ticket for her
car, but then uses the road to go to and from work
on only nine days. How much more (or less)
would she have spent had she purchased single
tickets instead?

  a. $44 less   **b.** $8 less   **c.** The same
  d. $8 more   **e.** $44 more

FIGURE 23: **Temperature at midday °C**

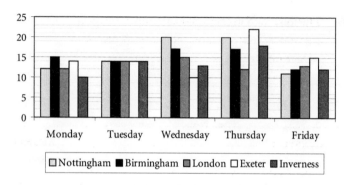

Practice questions

....

QUESTION

ANSWER

341. What was the average midday temperature on
Wednesday across the five cities?

a. 13°C   **b.** 14°C   **c.** 15°C
d. 16°C   **e.** 17°C

....

QUESTION

ANSWER

342. What was the average temperature in Inverness on
Tuesday?

a. 13°C   **b.** 14°C   **c.** 15°C
d. 16°C   **e.** Cannot Say

....

QUESTION | **ANSWER**

343. If the historical average midday temperature for this week in Exeter is 16°C, how does this week's average midday temperature compare?

a. 2°C lower   **b.** 1°C lower   **c.** The same
d. 1°C higher   **e.** 2°C higher

QUESTION | **ANSWER**

344. If, after Friday, the temperature in Nottingham increases every day by 1.5°C, by which day the following week will the midday temperature be in excess of 20°C?

a. Tuesday   **b.** Wednesday   **c.** Thursday
d. Friday   **e.** Saturday

QUESTION | **ANSWER**

345. Which city showed the greatest variation in midday temperature across the week?

a. Nottingham   **b.** Birmingham   **c.** London
d. Exeter   **e.** Inverness

QUESTION | **ANSWER**

346. For how many cities was the average midday temperature across the week in excess of 14°C?

a. 1   **b.** 2   **c.** 3
d. 4   **e.** All of them

FIGURE 24: **Employment Statistics**

Country	Total employed (1000s) Men	Women	Agriculture % of total employed	Number of fatal accidents	Mining % of total employed	Number of fatal accidents
A	2,070	1,670	14.3	25	9.1	33
B	2,310	1,715	16.2	27	6.8	98
C	1,250	1,050	12.7	8	4.4	11
D	2,310	1,230	15.1	16	7.5	4
E	5,050	3,900	18.5	136	8.2	246

Practice questions

QUESTION   ANSWER

347. Which two countries have almost the same
number of people employed in Agriculture?

    a. A and B   **b.** A and C   **c.** A and D
    d. B and D   **e.** C and D

QUESTION   ANSWER

348. In Country A approximately how many people
work in Agriculture and Mining combined?

    a. 871,000   **b.** 873,000   **c.** 874,000
    d. 875,000   **e.** 876,000

QUESTION   ANSWER

349. If 25% of workers in Agriculture in Country D are
women, approximately how many women work in
Agriculture in Country D?

a. 134,000   **b.** 268,000   **c.** 402,000
d. 534,000   **e.** Cannot say

QUESTION   ANSWER

350. Per 1,000 workers, what is the fatality rate in
Country B's mining industry?

a. 0.28   **b.** 0.32   **c.** 0.36
d. 0.40   **e.** 0.44

QUESTION   ANSWER

351. If the target fatality rate in Mining for Country A
is 0.05 per thousand workers, by what proportion
would the fatality rate need to be reduced?

a. 0.4   **b.** 0.5   **c.** 0.6
d. 0.7   **e.** Cannot Say

QUESTION   ANSWER

352. Which country has the second lowest fatality rate
in Mining?

a. Country A   **b.** Country B   **c.** Country C
d. Country D   **e.** Country E

Practice test 4

FIGURE 25: Expenses per year for Company A

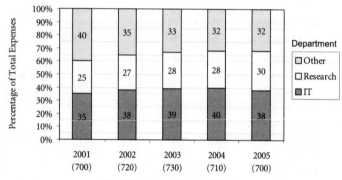

<hr />

QUESTION   ANSWER

353. In which year did Research account for the highest
percentage of expenses?

    a. 2001   **b.** 2002   **c.** 2003

    d. 2004   **e.** 2005

<hr />

QUESTION   ANSWER

354. In 2003 what were the total expenses in IT?

    a. £280,800   **b.** £284,700   **c.** £292,600

    d. £293,500   **e.** £294,400

QUESTION   ANSWER

355. What were the combined expenses of the 'other' departments over the five years?

a. £1,220,000   b. £1,222,000   c. £1,224,100

d. £1,226,000   e. £1,228,000

QUESTION   ANSWER

356. In which year were the expenses of the IT department the greatest?

a. 2001   b. 2002   c. 2003

d. 2004   e. 2005

QUESTION   ANSWER

357. If the advertising department accounted for 30% of the 'other' departments in 2001 and then 25% in both 2002 and 2003, over these three years, how much was spent on expenses in advertising?

a. £201,125   b. £203,700   c. £205,750

d. £207,225   e. £209,550

QUESTION   ANSWER

358. From 2005 to 2006, total expenses rose by 1.5% and the percentage of the expenses from 'other' departments remained constant. If the ratio of expenses in IT to expenses in research was 1.5:1, what were the total expenses in IT in 2006?

a. £289,800   b. £289,821   c. £289,842

d. £289,863   e. £289,884

FIGURE 26: **Carbon Dioxide Emissions (in million kg)**

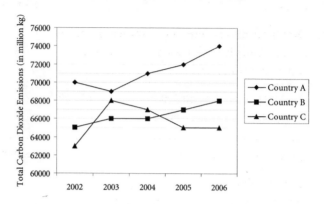

QUESTION	ANSWER

359. How many million kg of carbon dioxide emissions were produced by all three countries in 2002?

a. 195,000   **b.** 196,000   **c.** 197,000

d. 198,000   **e.** 199,000

QUESTION	ANSWER

360. What was the ratio of carbon dioxide emissions of Country A to Country C in 2005?

a. 1.10:1   **b.** 1.11:1   **c.** 1.12:1

d. 1.13:1   **e.** 1.14:1

QUESTION   ANSWER

361. Over the five years, on average how many million
kg of carbon dioxide emissions were produced
each year by Country B?

a. 66,000   **b.** 66,200   **c.** 66,400
d. 66,600   **e.** 66,800

QUESTION   ANSWER

362. In 2004 carbon dioxide emissions per capita in
Country C were 2,830 kg. What was the
population of Country C in 2004?

a. 23.45 million **b.** 23.56 million **c.** 23.67 million
d. 23.78 million **e.** 23.89 million

QUESTION   ANSWER

363. What was the percentage increase in carbon
dioxide emissions of Country A from 2003 to
2005?

a. 1.4%   **b.** 2.2%   **c.** 2.9%
d. 3.6%   **e.** 4.3%

QUESTION   ANSWER

364. In which year did the carbon dioxide emissions
from these three countries contribute the highest
percentage to world carbon dioxide emissions?

a. 2003   **b.** 2004   **c.** 2005
d. 2006   **e.** Cannot Say

FIGURE 27: **Average commuting times of those driving to work (one way)**

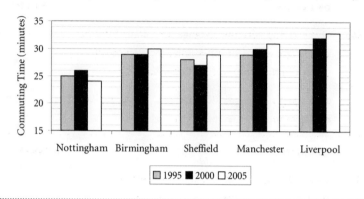

....

QUESTION   ANSWER

365. In 2000 what was the average one-way commuter
driving time across all five cities?

   a. 28 minutes 8 seconds
   b. 28 minutes 48 seconds
   c. 29 minutes 18 seconds
   d. 29 minutes 38 seconds
   e. Cannot Say

....

QUESTION   ANSWER

366. In 2005 a driver in Manchester took 5% longer
than the average one-way commuting time. How
long was their commute?

   a. 32 minutes 11 seconds
   b. 32 minutes 22 seconds
   c. 32 minutes 33 seconds
   d. 32 minutes 44 seconds
   e. 32 minutes 55 seconds

....

QUESTION   ANSWER

367. If the average driving distance for a commuter in
Birmingham was 16 miles one way, how much
faster did they travel in 2000 than 2005?

   a. 1.1 mph   **b.** 1.2 mph   **c.** 1.3 mph
   d. 1.4 mph   **e.** 1.5 mph

QUESTION   ANSWER

368. In which year was the average commuting time
the longest in Nottingham?

   a. 1990   **b.** 1995   **c.** 2000
   d. 2005   **e.** Cannot Say

QUESTION   ANSWER

369. If the annual average increase in the one-way
commuting time was constant in Sheffield from
2000 to 2005 what was the average commuting
time in 2003?

   a. 27 minutes 55 seconds
   b. 28 minutes 12 seconds
   c. 28 minutes 19 seconds
   d. 28 minutes 27 seconds
   e. 28 minutes 32 seconds

QUESTION   ANSWER

370. Which city had the second greatest percentage
change in commuting time from 1995 to 2005?

   a. Nottingham   **b.** Birmingham   **c.** Sheffield
   d. Manchester   **e.** Liverpool

FIGURE 28: Company X's Revenue Based on Office Location

Office	Total Revenue ('000 £s)	Total Sales Revenue ('000 £s)	Total Expenditure ('000 £s)	Cost of Staff ('000 £s)	Number of Staff
Birmingham	700	645	680	508	17
Bristol	683	604	672	347	12
Edinburgh	722	662	696	545	19
Liverpool	710	654	692	469	16
Nottingham	708	639	688	398	14

....

QUESTION   ANSWER

371. What was the overall profit across all five offices?

   a. £95,000   **b.** £1,250,000   **c.** £2,216,000
   d. £2,945,000   **e.** £3,523,000

....

QUESTION   ANSWER

372. By what percentage will sales revenue in Bristol
      need to improve if it is to exceed that in Liverpool
      next year assuming that sales revenue in Liverpool
      remains constant?

   a. 7.60%   **b.** 7.70%   **c.** 7.90%
   d. 8.10%   **e.** 8.30%

....

| QUESTION | ANSWER |

373. In which office did the total sales revenue account for the highest percentage of total revenue?

a. Birmingham   **b.** Bristol   **c.** Edinburgh
d. Liverpool   **e.** Nottingham

| QUESTION | ANSWER |

374. What was the ratio of total expenditure in Edinburgh to that in Birmingham?

a. 0.98:1   **b.** 1.00:1   **c.** 1.02:1
d. 1.04:1   **e.** 1.06:1

| QUESTION | ANSWER |

375. What was the cost of staff as a percentage of total expenditure across all five offices?

a. 65.0%   **b.** 66.1%   **c.** 67.2%
d. 68.3%   **e.** 69.4%

| QUESTION | ANSWER |

376. Approximately, what was the average cost of each staff member across all five offices?

a. £25,020   **b.** £26,031   **c.** £27,042
d. £28,053   **e.** £29,064

Practice test 5

FIGURE 29: Office paper

Type of Paper	Standard price (per pack)	Bulk price (more than 15 packs) (per pack)	Number of sheets per pack	Pack weight (grams)
A4	£6.50	£5.50	500	1250
Letter	£6.99	£5.99	512	1150
Foolscap	£7.50	£6.50	512	1350
A5	£3.00	£2.50	250	310
A3	£7.99	£6.99	500	2500

....

QUESTION   ANSWER

377.   How much will 20 packs of A4 paper cost?

   a. £110   **b.** £115   **c.** £120
   d. £125   **e.** £130

....

QUESTION   ANSWER

378.   What is the cost of 20 packs of both A3 and A5 paper?

   a. £165.00   **b.** £170.00   **c.** £189.80
   d. £199.90   **e.** £209.80

....

QUESTION   ANSWER

379. What is the difference in the paper cost of printing 500 sheets using A5 rather than A4 paper?

a. £0.50 cheaper   b. £3.50 cheaper
c. The same   d. £0.50 more costly
e. £3.50 more costly

QUESTION   ANSWER

380. Which type of paper offers the greatest proportional discount for bulk purchases?

a. A4   b. Letter   c. Foolscap
d. A5   e. A3

QUESTION   ANSWER

381. When 25 packs or more in total are purchased, an additional 12.5% discount is applied to the whole order. How much will 40 packs of Foolscap and 10 packs of Letter paper cost?

a. £274.28   b. £288.66   c. £297.42
d. £312.25   e. £329.90

QUESTION   ANSWER

382. Assuming that the packaging for a pack of paper has negligible mass, how much would 300 sheets of A4 paper and 625 sheets of A3 paper weigh?

a. 3,500 g   b. 3,625 g   c. 3,750 g
d. 3,875 g   e. Cannot say

FIGURE 30: **IT Investment**

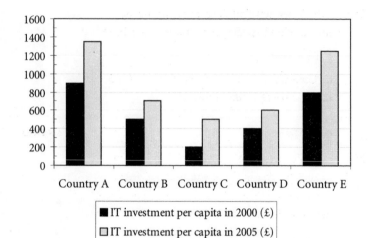

383. By what percentage did the IT investment per
capita increase from 2000 to 2005 in Country C?

    a. 100%   **b.** 150%   **c.** 200%

    d. 2.50%   **e.** None of these

384. In 2000 the IT investment per capita in Country B
was approximately what percentage of the IT
investment per capita in Country A?

    a. 48%   **b.** 52%   **c.** 56%

    d. 60%   **e.** 64%

QUESTION   ANSWER

385. Which country had the greatest proportional increase in IT spend per capita between 2000 and 2005?

a. Country A   **b.** Country B   **c.** Country C
d. Country D   **e.** Country E

QUESTION   ANSWER

386. If the IT investment per capita increases from 2005 to 2008 by 10% in Country C and by 15% in Country D, how much more is the IT investment per capita in Country D than in Country C in 2008?

a. £130   **b.** £120   **c.** £110
d. £100   **e.** None of these

QUESTION   ANSWER

387. If the population in Country E increased from 5.7 to 6.0 million from 2000 to 2005, approximately how much more was the total investment on IT made in Country E in 2005 compared to 2000?

a. £2.94 million   **b.** £29.4 million
c. £294 million   **d.** £2,940 million
e. £29,400 million

QUESTION   ANSWER

388. In 2000, what was the ratio of IT investment per capita in Country C to that in Country E?

a. 1:4   **b.** 3:4   **c.** 4:3
d. 4:1   **e.** None of these

FIGURE 31: **Online banking helpline – Support calls over a weekend**

Total number of calls = 960
Twice as many calls received Saturday as Sunday

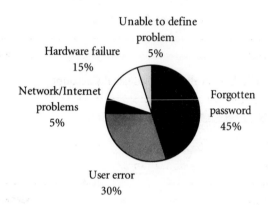

Unable to define
problem
5%

Hardware failure
15%

Network/Internet
problems
5%

Forgotten
password
45%

User error
30%

....

QUESTION ANSWER

389. How many calls in total were received on the
Saturday?

    a. 320   **b.** 480   **c.** 640

    d. 960   **e.** Cannot say

....

QUESTION ANSWER

390. How many calls on the Saturday were classified as
due to a hardware failure?

    a. 48   **b.** 96   **c.** 144

    d. 192   **e.** Cannot say

....

QUESTION   ANSWER

391. How many calls over the weekend were classified as
due to either user error or a forgotten password?

    a. 660   **b.** 680   **c.** 700

    d. 720   **e.** None of these

QUESTION   ANSWER

392. If support calls over the weekend usually account
for 40% of the week's calls, how many calls would
be predicted for that week in total?

    a. 2,400   **b.** 2,450   **c.** 2,500

    d. 2,550   **e.** None of these

QUESTION   ANSWER

393. If, on Saturday, the number of support calls
represented 0.16% of the overall number of hits to
the website, how many hits were there in total?

    a. 400   **b.** 4,000   **c.** 40,000

    d. 400,000   **e.** 4,000,000

QUESTION   ANSWER

394. If, the following weekend, the number of calls
classified as 'Network/Internet problems' and
'Unable to define problem' both doubled, while
the other calls did not change, how many calls
were there in total?

    a. 1,008   **b.** 1,056   **c.** 1,104

    d. 1,152   **e.** 1,200

FIGURE 32: **Staff Costs at Intertech Group**

Region	Number of Employees		Total Staff Costs (£ millions)	
	Sales	Operations	Sales	Operations
China	30	140	0.24	1.20
Europe	257	845	8.96	17.60
The Middle East	50	300	1.12	7.20
South East Asia	53	318	0.84	6.50
The Americas	220	1097	4.50	23.10

(All employees are categorized as either sales or operations)

....

QUESTION   ANSWER

395. Next year, it is planned to transfer 200 operations
jobs from Europe to South East Asia.
Assuming the staff costs per person for each
region remain unchanged, what approximate cost
saving would that generate?

a. 77,590   **b.** 77,600   **c.** 77,610

d. 77,620   **e.** 77,630

....

QUESTION   ANSWER

396. Last year, the China region had only two-thirds of
the number of Sales staff it has now and only three
quarters of the number of Operations staff it has
now. By approximately what percentage did staff
in the China region increase between last year and
this year?

a. 36%   **b.** 40%   **c.** 44%

d. 48%   **e.** 52%

....

QUESTION   ANSWER

397. For which two regions are the ratios of employees in sales to those in operations the same?

a. China and Europe
b. China and the Americas
c. The Middle East and the Americas
d. The Middle East and South East Asia
e. None of these

QUESTION   ANSWER

398. In which region is the cost per employee in operations the highest?

a. China   b. Europe
c. The Middle East   d. South East Asia
e. The Americas

QUESTION   ANSWER

399. Taking both Europe and the Americas combined, what is the approximate average staff cost per employee?

a. £21,050   b. £21,150   c. £21,250
d. £21,350   e. £21,450

QUESTION   ANSWER

400. Sales staff make up what proportion of the staff complement for Intertech Group?

a. 14.29%   b. 16.38%   c. 18.43%
d. 20.57%   e. 22.60%

Further reading

We hope that now you have read this book you have a good understanding of what numerical tests are about and that you understand some of the things you can do in order to improve your performance. If you have gone through all the practice questions included here it means that you have practised 400 numerical questions. This will not only improve your performance but should also increase your confidence in solving numerical tests.

If you feel you want to practise some more sample questions or if you want to have a go at filling out tests online, there are a few websites you could use. These are links to companies that create psychometric tests, and you can access their practice tests and also look for other information that may interest you.

http://www.kenexa.com
http://www.morrisby.com
http://www.shldirect.com/shldirect-homepage/SHLDirect-1.asp
http://www.psychometrics-uk.com/bapt.html
http://www.mensa.org/workout2.php
http://www.ets.org/
http://www.psychometric-success.com/
http://www.savilleconsulting.com/
http://www.assessmentday.co.uk/
http://www.ase-solutions.co.uk/

If you are interested in reading about other types of psychometric tests, we would recommend:

Joanna Moutafi and Ian Newcombe, *Perfect Psychometric Test Results* (London, 2007)

Helen Baron, *Perfect Personality Profiles* (London, 2007)

Also, if you want to improve your performance in other parts of the selection process – for example, if you want to improve your CV or to improve your performance at interviews – you could also read:

Max Eggert, *Perfect Interview* (London, 2003)

Max Eggert, *Perfect Answers to Interview Questions* (London, 2005)

Max Eggert, *Perfect CV* (London, 2003)

Answers to practice questions

Question	Answer
Simple calculations	
1.	88
2.	75
3.	100
4.	81
5.	47
6.	82
7.	59
8.	37
9.	26
10.	45
11.	6
12.	61
13.	19
14.	53
15.	25
16.	33
17.	56
18.	54
19.	60
20.	45
21.	12
22.	9

Question	Answer
23.	9
24.	12
25.	7
26.	7
27.	12
28.	28
29.	9
30.	7
Numerical estimation	
31.	c
32.	d
33.	e
34.	b
35.	c
36.	d
37.	a
38.	d
39.	b
40.	e
41.	c
42.	d
43.	b

Question	Answer		Question	Answer
44.	a		70.	a
45.	b		71.	e
46.	c		72.	a
47.	a		73.	c
48.	e		74.	b
49.	e		75.	c
50.	a		76.	d
			77.	d
			78.	e

Rounding off

51.	68.44
52.	8.24
53.	0.62
54.	0.74
55.	5.29
56.	14.8
57.	7.2
58.	3.0
59.	4.3
60.	6.4

Percentages

79.	33.1%
80.	1035.0%
81.	0.9%
82.	12.7%
83.	12054.9%
84.	0.26
85.	0.13
86.	0.89
87.	2.20
88.	1.30
89.	0.157
90.	0.147
91.	0.243
92.	0.556
93.	1.028
94.	b
95.	a
96.	c
97.	d
98.	b

Averages

61.	a
62.	c
63.	e
64.	d
65.	b
66.	b
67.	e
68.	d
69.	c

Question	Answer	Question	Answer
99.	e	130.	b
100.	a	131.	c
101.	c	132.	d
102.	b	133.	a
103.	c	134.	b
104.	b	135.	c
105.	a	136.	d
106.	a	137.	a
107.	d	138.	e
108.	e	139.	d
109.	d	140.	b
110.	a	141.	d
111.	d	142.	e
112.	b	143.	c
113.	e	144.	b
114.	c	145.	b
115.	b	146.	a
116.	d	147.	c
117.	c	148.	d
118.	a	149.	e
119.	d	150.	d
120.	c	151.	d
121.	e	152.	c
122.	b	153.	a
123.	d	154.	a
124.	d		
125.	d	**Ratios**	
126.	c	155.	c
127.	a	156.	b
128.	b	157.	d
129.	d	158.	e

Question	Answer		Question	Answer
159.	a		188.	b
160.	b		189.	a
161.	a		190.	d
162.	b		191.	b
163.	e		192.	c
164.	d			
165.	a		**Figure 6**	
166.	c		193.	b
167.	b		194.	c
168.	b		195.	e
169.	d		196.	b
170.	e		197.	d
171.	c		198.	e
172.	e		199.	e
173.	c		200.	e
174.	b			
175.	c		**Figure 7**	
176.	b		201.	c
177.	a		202.	b
178.	d		203.	d
179.	a		204.	b
180.	c		205.	e
181.	d		206.	b
182.	c			
183.	a		**Figure 8**	
184.	a		207.	d
			208.	c
Figure 1 (repeated)			209.	a
185.	b		210.	c
186.	d		211.	d
187.	c		212.	b

Question	Answer		Question	Answer
Figure 9			**Number sequences**	
213.	e		237.	c
214.	e		238.	b
215.	d		239.	d
216.	a		240.	b
217.	d		241.	a
218.	c		242.	c
			243.	e
Figure 10			244.	c
219.	b		245.	d
220.	a		246.	c
221.	b		247.	c
222.	c		248.	e
223.	b		249.	c
224.	c		250.	e
			251.	d
Figure 11			252.	a
225.	b		253.	c
226.	c		254.	d
227.	c		255.	a
228.	d		256.	a
229.	e		257.	c
230.	e		258.	b
			259.	e
Figure 12			260.	d
231.	d			
232.	a		**Other non-graphical questions**	
233.	c		261.	c
234.	e		262.	e
235.	d		263.	a
236.	e		264.	b

Question	Answer	Question	Answer
265.	d	294.	b
266.	b	295.	d
267.	e	296.	c
268.	b	297.	d
269.	b	298.	a
270.	d	299.	b
271.	b	300.	b
272.	c	301.	a
273.	b	302.	e
274.	d	303.	c
275.	a	304.	c
276.	d		
277.	d	**Practice test 2**	
278.	c	305.	b
279.	b	306.	a
280.	a	307.	e
		308.	d
Practice test 1		309.	a
281.	d	310.	b
282.	c	311.	c
283.	a	312.	e
284.	c	313.	c
285.	b	314.	d
286.	e	315.	d
287.	d	316.	a
288.	c	317.	a
289.	d	318.	a
290.	b	319.	b
291.	e	320.	d
292.	a	321.	e
293.	e	322.	d

Question	Answer		Question	Answer
323.	d		352.	a
324.	c			
325.	e		**Practice test 4**	
326.	b		353.	e
327.	a		354.	b
328.	d		355.	c
			356.	c
Practice test 3			357.	d
329.	c		358.	e
330.	a		359.	d
331.	b		360.	b
332.	e		361.	c
333.	e		362.	c
334.	c		363.	e
335.	d		364.	e
336.	a		365.	b
337.	d		366.	c
338.	e		367.	a
339.	b		368.	e
340.	b		369.	b
341.	c		370.	a
342.	e		371.	a
343.	b		372.	e
344.	d		373.	a
345.	d		374.	c
346.	c		375.	b
347.	c		376.	e
348.	d			
349.	a		**Practice test 5**	
350.	c		377.	a
351.	b		378.	c

Question	Answer	Question	Answer
379.	a	390.	e
380.	d	391.	d
381.	b	392.	a
382.	d	393.	d
383.	b	394.	b
384.	c	395.	e
385.	c	396.	a
386.	e	397.	d
387.	d	398.	c
388.	a	399.	b
389.	c	400.	c

Perfect Psychometric Test Results

Joanna Moutafi and Ian Newcombe

All you need to get it right first time

- Have you been asked to sit a psychometric test?
- Do you want guidance on the sorts of questions you'll be asked?
- Do you want to make sure you perform to the best of your abilities?

Perfect Psychometric Test Results is the ideal guide for anyone who wants to secure their ideal job. Written by a team from Kenexa, one of the UK's leading compilers of psychometric tests, it explains how each test works, gives helpful pointers on how to get ready, and provides professionally constructed sample questions for you to try out at home. It also contains an in-depth section on online testing – the route that more and more recruiters are choosing to take. Whether you're a graduate looking to take the first step on the career ladder, or you're planning an all-important job change, *Perfect Psychometric Test Results* has everything you need to make sure you stand out from the competition.

The Perfect series is a range of practical guides that give clear and straightforward advice on everything from getting your first job to choosing your baby's name. Written by experienced authors offering tried-and-tested tips, each book contains all you need to get it right first time.

BOOKS

Perfect Personality Profiles

Helen Baron

All you need to make a great impression

- Have you been asked to complete a personality questionnaire?
- Do you need guidance on the sorts of questions you'll be asked?
- Do you want to make sure you show yourself in your best light?

Perfect Personality Profiles is essential reading for anyone who needs to find out more about psychometric profiling. Including everything from helpful pointers on how to get ready to professionally constructed sample questions for you to try out at home, it walks you through every aspect of preparing for a test. Whether you're a graduate looking to take the first step on the career ladder, or you're planning an all-important job change, *Perfect Personality Profiles* has everything you need to make sure you stand out from the competition.

BOOKS

Perfect CV

Max Eggert

All you need to get it right first time

- Are you determined to succeed in your job search?
- Do you need guidance on how to make a great first impression?
- Do you want to make sure your CV stands out?

Bestselling *Perfect CV* is essential reading for anyone who's applying for jobs. Written by a leading HR professional with years of experience, it explains what recruiters are looking for, gives practical advice about how to show yourself in your best light, and provides real-life examples to help you improve your CV. Whether you're a graduate looking to take the first step on the career ladder, or you're planning an all-important job change, *Perfect CV* will help you stand out from the competition.

BOOKS

Perfect Interview

Max Eggert

All you need to get it right first time

- Are you determined to succeed in your job search?
- Do you want to make sure you have the edge on the other candidates?
- Do you want to find out what interviewers are *really* looking for?

Perfect Interview is an invaluable guide for anyone who's applying for jobs. Written by a leading HR professional with years of experience in the field, it explains how interviews are constructed, gives practical advice about how to show yourself in your best light, and provides real-life examples to help you practise at home. Whether you're a graduate looking to take the first step on the career ladder, or you're planning an all-important job change, *Perfect Interview* will help you stand out from the competition.

BOOKS

Order more titles in the *Perfect* series
from your local bookshop, or have them delivered
direct to your door by Bookpost.

☐ Perfect Answers to Interview Questions	Max Eggert	9781844134601	£6.99
☐ Perfect Babies' Names	Rosalind Fergusson	9781905211661	£5.99
☐ Perfect Best Man	George Davidson	9781905211661	£5.99
☐ Perfect CV	Max Eggert	9781905211739	£7.99
☐ Perfect Interview	Max Eggert	9781905211746	£7.99
☐ Perfect Personality Profiles	Helen Baron	9781905211821	£7.99
☐ Perfect Psychometric Test Results	Joanna Moutafi and Ian Newcombe	9781905211678	£7.99
☐ Perfect Pub Quiz	David Pickering	9781905211692	£6.99
☐ Perfect Punctuation	Stephen Curtis	9781905211685	£5.99
☐ Perfect Readings for Weddings	Jonathan Law	9781905211098	£6.99
☐ Perfect Wedding Speeches and Toasts	George Davidson	9781905211777	£5.99

Free post and packing
Overseas customers allow £2 per paperback

Phone: 01624 677237

Post: Random House Books
c/o Bookpost, PO Box 29, Douglas, Isle of Man IM99 1BQ

Fax: 01624 670 923

email: <u>bookshop@enterprise.net</u>

Cheques (payable to Bookpost) and credit cards accepted

Prices and availability subject to change without notice.
Allow 28 days for delivery.
When placing your order, please state if you do not
wish to receive any additional information.

www.randomhouse.co.uk